LEGENDS OF THE PHILADELPHIA PHILLIES

ROBERT GORDON

www.SportsPublishingLLC.com

ISBN: 1-58261-810-0

Publishers: Peter L. Bannon and Joseph J. Bannon Sr.
Senior managing editor: Susan M. Moyer
Acquisitions editor: Dean Reinke
Developmental editor: Noah Amstadter
Art director: K. Jeffrey Higgerson
Book design: Heidi Norsen
Dust jacket design: Dustin J. Hubbart
Project manager: Dustin J. Hubbart
Imaging: Kenneth J. O'Brien, Heidi Norsen and Dustin J. Hubbart
Photo editor: Erin Linden-Levy
Vice president of sales and marketing: Kevin King
Media and promotions managers:
      Kelley Brown, regional marketing manager
      Randy Fouts, national marketing manager
      Maurey Williamson, print marketing manager

Printed in the United States

Sports Publishing L.L.C.
804 North Neil Street
Champaign, IL 61820

Phone: 1-877-424-2665
Fax: 217-363-2073
Web site: www.SportsPublishingLLC.com

To my Dad and the Eigners—Without the Phillies, would Philly be?

Without Aunt Mary, would Ocean City be?

Thank you for endless summers.

CONTENTS

INTRODUCTION vi

The Fightin' Phils 1

Bobby Abreu 6

Dick Allen 10

Richie Ashburn 14

Steve Bedrosian 20

Johnny Callison 24

Steve Carlton 28

Dave Cash 34

Larry Christenson 38

Clay Dalrymple 42

Darren Daulton 46

Jim Eisenreich 52

Del Ennis 56

Bill Giles 60

Tony Gonzalez 64

Al Holland 68

Dave Hollins 72

Pete Incaviglia   78

Harry Kalas   82

Jim Konstanty   86

Mike Lieberthal   90

Art Mahaffey   96

Gary Matthews   100

Maje   106

Tug McGraw   110

Dave Raymond   116

Robin Roberts   120

Mike Schmidt   126

Bobby Shantz   132

Jim Thome   136

Milt Thompson   142

Mitch Williams   146

INTRODUCTION

This book is *not* a tired, tiring roundup of the usual suspects punctuated with the usual stories about them. The litany of sanctioned Phillie legends starts with Al Reach, Harry Wright, Ed Delahanty, Sliding Billy Hamilton, and Elmer Flick, then rolls merrily along with Sherry Magee, Grover Cleveland Alexander, Eppa Rixey, Chuck Klein, Lefty O'Doul, etc.

Great names all—names that resonate a roll call of bona fide Phillie *greats*. But none of them are in the collection of Phillie legends you now hold in your hand (the ones you are eagerly preparing to read or purchase or vice versa). This book regales Phillie *legends*, not Phillie *greats*. Legends and greats are not necessarily the same—not by a long shot. Look at it this way.

Grover Cleveland Alexander is a great. The guy won 373 games. He threw 16 shutouts in a single season. How great is that? Forget shutouts—our 2004 Fightins didn't have a single 17-game winner on the staff. So everyone pretty much would have to accord Grover status as a great. Archibald "Moonlight" Graham, on the other hand, is not a *great*. His record, or lack of record, attests to that. It's hard to be a great when you never even stepped to the plate in the majors. But Moonlight *is* a legend. In fact, he's a bigger legend at this point than old Grover the Great. But don't take my word for it. Test out the hypothesis yourself. Ask several of

your baseball-fanatic friends how many games Grover won. Then ask them how many at-bats "Moonlight" had. The answers will shed more light on the great/legend distinction than you've ever shed on the great taste/less filling conundrum.

Some of the people posited as legends in this book are so only in the minds of Phillie fans. Some I confess, are probably legends only in my mind. Again, such is the nature of the term "legend"—a claim, in contrast to the term "great," that can be staked as legitimately by not-so-greats as greats.

Again, this book is not a roundup of the usual suspects. To be sure, greats like Mike Schmidt, Steve Carlton, Richie Ashburn, Tug McGraw, and Robin Roberts *do* appear. That's because these five are also legends. Not only are they legends, they are legends within relatively recent memory who performed in front of the potential readers of this book.

Legends of the Philadelphia Phillies focuses on Phillie people from the second half of the twentieth century till the present. Every chapter profiles a ballplayer or some other member of the Phillies organization who is still alive. There are four notable exceptions; namely Richie Ashburn, Del Ennis, Jim Konstanty, and Tug McGraw—who are all deceased. However even the most marginal Phillie fan would concur that this foursome merits inclusion in any book of Phillies legends.

In writing the book, I conducted extensive interviews with ex-Phils, current Phils, and front-office personnel. To ferret out fresher anecdotes and tall tales, I sought out various non-ballplayers as well—the close friends and confidants of many of the players profiled. Their insights add fresh color that should whet the interest of both the voracious and casual reader of "Phillies stuff" as well as baseball fans everywhere.

You'll find a chapter on Bobby Shantz even though Shantz pitched less than half a season for the Phils. He is included because he happened to be front and center during the most horrendous meltdown Pennsylvania ever suffered this side of Three Mile Island. Clay Dalrymple, who did not have a particularly distinguished career statistically, is profiled because the Dalrymple name, presumably eroded by time, has been popping up on the silver screen in recent years.

Dalrymple played almost a decade in Philly. Like Shantz, however, some of the other legends presented here strutted and fretted but briefly on the Philly diamond. Yet their stays were full of sound and fury where they garnered honors like Cy Young Awards, MVPs, and Rolaids Relief Man Awards.

A number of the legends profiled here endowed the Philly sport scene with evocative nicknames like Putt Putt, Action Dog, Bedrock, Mr. T, and Sarge, to name a few.

Having a cool nickname is a big step toward achieving "legend" status. So does being a fan favorite as many of the legends were and remain.

Some legends hang out outside the lines. The original Phillie Phanatic gives the inside scoop on his wacky job. Harry Kalas rekindles his halcyon Hawaii and Houston days, where he learned his chops as a broadcaster—and perhaps as a vaudevillian. Bill Giles is all smiles as he recounts some of his favorite promotions.

Three new kids on the Phillies block are profiled: Bobby Abreu, Jim Thome, and Mike Lieberthal, In counterpoint to these neophyte legends, you'll reminisce with a Phillies front-office guy whose tenure stretches back to the Truman Administration.

In a word (or several), this book is a compendium of Phillies lore that brushes the life of all the current generations of Phillie fans. It's chock full of facts, information, and anecdotes about various people who have represented Philly's hometown team for the past half-century. Read on and enjoy a nostalgic and often humorous look at the boys who have peopled the summers of your life.

—Robert Gordon
March 2005

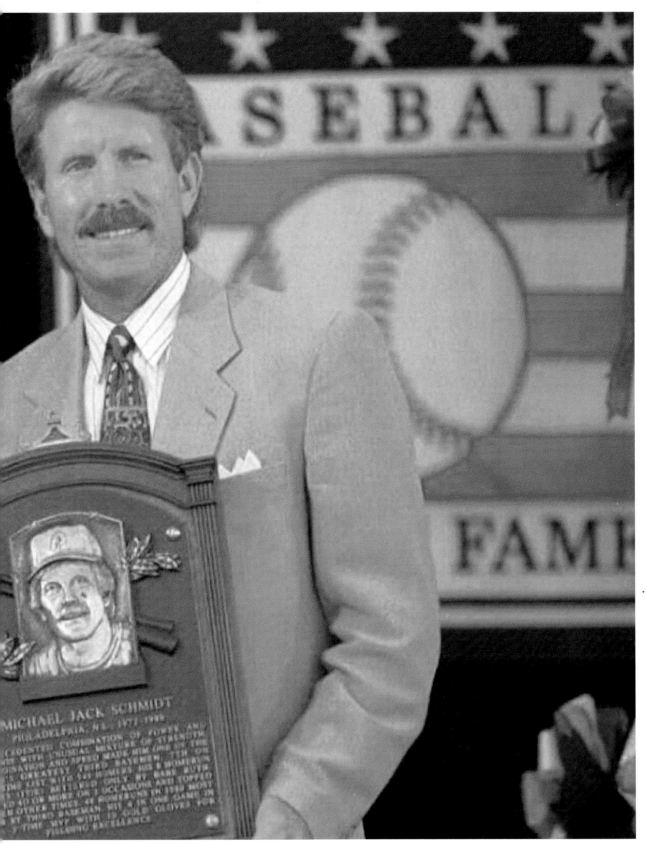

THE FIGHTIN' PHILS

Evidently when a door in Massachusetts closes, another opens in Philadelphia. Young Bostonian Benjamin Franklin started the trend. Ben left Beantown in the mid-18th century and ventured to Philadelphia, there to become his adopted city's most enduring symbol. A century and some change later, Cornelius McGillicuddy left the Boston area to become Connie Mack, Philly's most enduring sport figure—a man who managed a Philly team for more than half a century and tallied more victories than any baseball manager ever has or ever will. So when the struggling Worcester Ruby Red Legs flopped up in Massachusetts, it seems natural in history's unerring rear view mirror (where events appear more distant than they really were) that National League president A.G. Mills would court Philadelphia to replace the floundering New England franchise.

The National League was six years old at the time. Mills tapped Al Reach to colonize Philly. Reach, a left-handed throwing second baseman, played from 1871 to 1875 in the old National Association, the professional league generally recognized as the precursor to the National League. Reach was a natural for the job. He was a former baseball player, but he was also a successful entrepreneur who ran a profitable sporting goods business. Mills coveted Philadelphia, which he envisioned as a fertile professional sports market. History has proved Mills a visionary. The Philadelphia Phillies—the team born out of the Worcester ashes—is the longest-standing professional team with the same name in *any* US sport.

Original owner Reach was the one who dubbed his new team the Phillies. Reach said he chose the name because it "tells who we are and where we come from."

The Phillies actually did make one half-hearted attempt to change their name. In reality it was more an attempt to change their image. Their attempted image change took place in the forties—same as it does with most men. In the Phillies' case, that would be the 1940's. The Phils' new owner, Robert Carpenter, wanted to give his new club a shot of rhythm and blues, as Chuck Berry would say. Carpenter figured a name change would do the trick. The Phils changed their name to Blue Jays—unofficially. Interestingly enough,

Left: Hall of Famer Ed Delahanty was one of the turn-of-the century Phillies stars that increased the team's popularity.
Courtesy of the Philadelphia Phillies

attendance that year (1943) skyrocketed to over 400,000 for the first time since 1916, the year after the franchise's first and only pennant to that point. Perhaps the spurt in attendance is better explained by the fact that the Phils did *not* finish in last place that year, as they had the five previous campaigns. In '43, they shot all the way up to next to last.

In any event, prior to the '43 season, the Phillies ran a contest to rename the team. Blue Jays was the winner. Fortunately the name never caught on (it's fortunate because the '93 World Series, Toronto versus Philadelphia, would have pitted Blue Jay against Blue Jay). The name change didn't stick. Philly fans never stopped calling their team the Phillies, so the team was, is, and will always remain the Phillies.

Now, back to Al Reach and his fledgling National League franchise. The year was 1883—the same year the first vaudeville theatre opened in Boston. Roselle, New Jersey became the first city to use overhead wires for electric service that year. And the Brooklyn Bridge opened—for traffic that is. Otherwise, it didn't open al la the Tacony Palmyra bridge.

The Phils' 1883 season got off to an inauspicious start on April 22 at Recreation Park when the Providence Grays beat them 6-5. The season went downhill from there. Reach's boys went on to lose another 80 games in recording a franchise-worst 17-81 record and a franchise-worst .173 winning (?) percentage.

After a horrendous debut like that, things could only get better—right? That was a test. If you answered yes, you probably listen to Tony Robbins tapes to and from work. You probably root for the Yankees, and you probably don't know what happened in 1964 in Philly. On the other hand, if you said no, you've probably undergone an IRS audit recently. Or you have teenage kids. Or you belong to Philly's largest demographic—the naysayers known as Phillie and Eagle rooters.

The answer to the question posed above is yes. Things *did* get better for the Phils. Harry Wright took over the helm and won more games (636) than any other Phillie manager in history except for Gene Mauch. Mauch's teams won nine more games than Wright's teams. The Hall of Fame sees a much greater difference between the two ex-Phillie skippers. The bust of Harry Wright is immortalized in the Hall of Fame while Mauch possesses a lifetime visitor's pass.

Throughout Wright's ten-year tenure, the Phils were contenders who never quite made it to the uppermost top. Their shortfall wasn't due to a dearth of talent. During the Wright era, several future Hall of Famers populated Philadelphia's lineup. The trend continued after Wright's departure. Ed Delahanty, Sam Thompson, Nap Lajoie, Elmer Flick, and Billy Hamilton—Hall of Famers all—starred for the Phils around the turn of the century. In fact, the Phils grew so popular with the local folk that they had to construct a brand new stadium not too many years after their arrival in Philly. Their first park, little more than a grandstand around a diamond, was called Recreation Park. In 1887, Reach built a new double-decker stadium that was mammoth for its era. He dubbed it the Huntingdon Grounds, which carried the hefty price tag of $101,000. Seating capacity was 12,500, substantially higher than the 1,500 capacity at Recreation Park.

The Phils had some down years as the nineteenth century turned. Then they gained some steam. They rumbled through the twentieth century's first decade but never thundered. They managed several first-division finishes, but never seriously contended.

When Nebraska rookie Grover Cleveland Alexander arrived in 1911, the Phils gained the oomph they needed to contend. Hopping aboard the Alexander train, the Phils chugged to their first NL pennant in 1915 under rookie manager Pat Moran. They jumped out to a promising start in the World Series, beating their American League opponent, the Boston Red Sox, 4-1, behind Alexander's dominant pitching. Unfortunately for the Phils, that win was all she wrote. They followed with four straight losses to the Bosox, and were destined (or cursed) not to win another World Series game until 1980. The 1915 Series marked an historic first in what has become a long-standing baseball tradition. Philly became the first city where a U.S. president attended a World Series game. President Woodrow Wilson was present in National League Park for Game 2.

After 1915, the Phils' fortunes declined precipitously. Boston had its Curse of the Bambino. However, Philadelphia might similarly claim a Curse of Pete Alexander. After winning the pennant in 1915 because of Alexander, the Phils finished runner-up in 1916, as Alexander rolled to 33 wins and an unprecedented 17 shutouts. The great righthander followed in 1917 with his third consecutive 30-win season, prompting the Phils to trade him. Apparently the Phils had a hunch he'd never win 30 again, and they were spot on. He never did. That's the good news. The bad news is that he did win 20-plus games three other seasons and tallied 183 victories in the '20s wearing Cub or Cardinal flannels. Immediately upon Alexander's departure,

the Phils plummeted to sixth place in 1918 and a last-place finish a year later. They would occupy last place throughout most of the '20s.

When the '30s dawned, the Phils packed loads of lumber into their lineup. Led by future

Ed Delahanty, Sam Thompson, Nap Lajoie, Elmer Flick, and Billy Hamilton— Hall of Famers all—starred for the Phils around the turn of the century. In fact, the Phils grew so popular with the local folk that they had to construct a brand new stadium.

Hall of Famer Chuck Klein, the Phils rapped out hits aplenty in the friendly confines of Baker Bowl, as the restored Huntingdon Grounds became known at some unspecified time after 1913. The original stadium had burned down in 1894 and was replaced at the same site. The new edifice was christened National League Park. However sometime during the 1913-1930 tenure of Phils owner William F. Baker, Baker Bowl assumed the name the defunct park has carried into history. Baker Bowl is what the defunct park has carried into history.

As much as the Phillies found Baker Bowl hitter-friendly, the opposition found it even moreso. Opponents rapped out even more hits than the Phillies in the Baker Bowl thanks to the Phils' woeful pitching staff. In 1930, Phils pitchers amassed a 6.72 ERA, highest in league history (note: claims by

Philly old-timers that policemen had to be stationed at the visiting team's bat-rack to prevent visiting-team regulars from rioting if second-stringers replaced them and cheated them out of an at-bat against Phillies pitchers appear unfounded). Meanwhile that same season, Phils batters topped the senior circuit with a lofty .315 team average. Nonetheless, the Phils finished last, 40 games behind the front-running Cubs. The stats add some teeth to that old saw about good pitching always beating good hitting—although Bob Veale, a former Pittsburgh pitcher, might have come closest to the mark when he observed that "Good pitching always beats good hitting, and vice versa."

Tops among Phillie batsmen were Chuck Klein and Lefty O'Doul. The latter was only a Phil for two seasons. In 1930, O'Doul recorded the top batting average of any Phillie in history, .398. In 1931, Klein sizzled in at .386 with Lefty not far behind at .383. The KO combo of Klein-O'Doul placed third and fourth among NL batsmen that year. In 1932, Klein won the National League MVP. The following year, Klein won the Triple Crown and did *not* win the MVP. The NL Award that year went to the New York Giants' Meal Ticket, Carl Hubbell. Hubbell was 23-12 for the first-place Giants. In 1933, Phillies accounted for 25 percent of the NL starters in the first ever All-Star game, as both Chuck Klein and shortstop Dick Bartell were selected. Not until

1947 would the Phils again place two starters in the mid-summer classic. Second-baseman Emil Verban and outfielder Harry "The Hat" Walker started that year.

The '30s were bleak for the Phils despite impressive offensive numbers. Besides Chuck Klein and Lefty O'Doul, Spud Davis hit .313, .326, .336, and .349 in consecutive seasons. Don Hurst hit .285, .304, .327, .305, .339 in consecutive seasons; Dick Bartell .289, .308, .271, and .310 in consecutive seasons; and Pincky Whitney .301, .327, .342, .287, .298 in consecutive seasons.

Impressive numbers, but the Phils finished in last place four times in the '30s. As the end of the decade neared, their offense turned anemic. Their pitchers got virtually no run support. One Phillie pitcher, Hugh Mulcahey, was nicknamed "Losing Pitcher" because the boxscore listed him as the "Losing Pitcher" so often. "Losing Pitcher" Mulcahey—a name that most PR firms would consider a liability in negotiation salary or campaigning for the All-Star team—was selected to the 1940 NL All-Star team—a tipoff that the offense was rather inept.

When Bob Carpenter bought the franchise in 1943, the Phils' fortunes slowly started to change. Carpenter fostered a business-like, systematized approach. He believed strong, integrated business organizations spawn winning teams. He created and nurtured a Phillies minor-league system for the first time in the

In 1950, Bob Carpenter's system and approach paid dividends. The Phillie Whiz Kids shocked the baseball world by besting Brooklyn's fabled Boys of Summer for the NL pennant.

club's history. Till Carpenter's arrival, the Phils had no minor league network. Carpenter also started paying bonus money to prospects like Robin Roberts and Curt Simmons.

In 1950, Carpenter's system and approach paid dividends. The Phillie Whiz Kids shocked the baseball world by besting Brooklyn's fabled Boys of Summer for the NL pennant. Unfortunately, the Yankees stifled the joy. The Bronx Bombers scored a four-game sweep in a low-scoring, tightly contested World Series. Every contest but the final one was decided by a run.

With the success of the Whiz Kids, Philadelphia boasted its first group of post-war baseball heroes. The Philadelphia Eagles had won the NFL championship in 1948 and '49. Thus to the Eagles' litany of local heroes—Steve Van Buren, Tommy Thompson, Chuck Bednarik, Pete Pihos, Vic Sears, and others—was added a new group of Phillies stars: Robin Roberts, Richie Ashburn, Del Ennis, Granny Hamner, Puddin' Head Jones, Russ Meyer, and others.

Unfortunately, injuries prevented the Whiz Kids from sustaining. As the '50s waned, the Phils faded. They were never able to catch Brooklyn or the New York Giants, who took off behind their young superstar Willie Mays. In the early '60s, Johnny Callison blasted into the Quaker City via the White Sox and anchored another good Phillies squad. By the mid-'60s, after acquiring Jim Bunning, Tony Gonzalez, Wes Covington, Cookie Rojas, and others, the Phils were bona fide contenders. In 1964, a year that will forever live in infamy in Philadelphia, the Phils lost a pennant they had firmly in their grasp. With a dozen games to play, they blew a six-and-a-half-game game lead. The debacle traumatized Philadelphians forever.

The team was in shambles by the end of the decade. The franchise breathed new life once the team moved to Veterans Stadium in 1971. A whole new cast of Phillies characters settled into the city. By 1976, Mike Schmidt, Steve Carlton, Garry Maddox, Larry Bowa, Bob Boone, Greg Luzinski, Tug McGraw, and others had led the Phils to their first division title since 1950. The Phils boasted their franchise-best (to this day) winning percentage (.623). The Phils won the division again in 1977 (with the identical .623 percentage) and 1978. Both years, they failed to take the NL flag. Finally in 1980, on the left wing of Tug McGraw, the Phils won their only World Series.

The Phils won the NL pennant again in 1983 behind Gary Matthews' sterling National League Championship Series performance. The Phils followed by winning the Series opener. Garry Maddox hit the game-winning home run in a 2-1 squeaker in an auspicious start. Unfortunately, they then followed the 1915 script to a tee, losing four in succession to Baltimore.

Ten years ensued after the '83 Series before the Phils again climbed to the top. Their most popular team ever—the 1993 "Beards, Bellies, and Biceps" squad of John Kruk, Lenny Dykstra, Darren Daulton, Curt Schilling, Dave Hollins, Milt Thompson, and others—bashed the Atlanta Braves in an exciting NLCS. The Phils went on to lose a heartbreaking Series to Toronto when Mitch Williams served up a walk-off homer to Joe Carter.

The '94 season ushered in down times for the remainder of the '90s. However, with the move on up to Citizens Bank Park, the team has again ascended as a National League power. Behind Jim Thome, Bobby Abreu, Randy Wolf, Pat Burrell, and Jimmy Rollins, the Phils have once again become one of baseball's better teams.

BOBBY ABREU

A new star showed up in the Philadelphia firmament in 2004. Actually, the star has been burning bright for years. Philly stargazers simply failed to notice. When Bobby Abreu was selected to the 2004 National League All-Star squad by fan vote, he finally enjoyed some measure of overdue recognition and affirmation.

Bobby Abreu had put up "star" stats for years, though he never received much national press. His numbers were steady and impressive. They weren't spectacular. Abreu wasn't slamming 50-plus homers a season like his more ballyhooed NL outfield peers. He wasn't hitting .350 and winning batting titles. But after six years of patrolling the Phils' outfield, Bobby's list of accomplishments are phenomenal.

For instance, ask any Phillies fan who tops the Phils' all-time list for on-base percentage. You're likely to hear a litany of guesses: Delahanty, Ashburn, Magee, Klein, Kruk, Dykstra, and Schmidt. They're all educated guesses. But they're all incorrect. The correct answer is Bobby Abreu.

In the minds of most fans, Bobby Abreu is an unlikely candidate for that honor. Yet going into

Born: March 11, 1974, Aragua, Venezuela
Position: Right Field
Uniform Number: 53
Years with the Phillies: 1998-current
Major League Stats (Through 2004): .305, 166 HR, 674 RBI
Honors:
• 2004 NL All-Star
• Named to the All Vet team (the only member of the current Phillies to be so honored)
• Ranks No. 1 on Phillies all-time list for On Base Percentage
• Named NL Player of the Week, May 28-June 3, 2001

the 2005 season, Abreu's lifetime .416 OBP ranks first among every player who ever donned Phillies' pinstripes. Likewise, Abreu's .308 lifetime batting average ranks number ten.

The Abreu name pops up all over the Phillies' all-time record book. He's number six in sacrifice flies, number seven in doubles, tied for fourth in intentional walks, number four in walks, number eight in stolen bases, number nine in home runs. He will soon enter the top ten in Phillie RBIs. In two more years, Abreu will crack the Phillies all-time top ten list in every offensive category except singles and triples. Meanwhile, defensively he ranks in the Phils' all-time top 20 in outfield assists.

Aside from his esteemed place in the Phillies record book, Abreu has joined a very exclusive club that includes three other all-time greats: Bobby Bonds, Barry Bonds, and Willie Mays. The members of this quartet are the only players ever to hit 20 homers and steal 20 bases for six consecutive seasons.

> # "I'm glad to see Bobby make the All-Star team and finally get some of the recognition he's earned," Larry Bowa comments. "Bobby has all the tools. He runs, hits, has a good arm, and has power. He doesn't do things spectacularly but he gets the job done every day."
>
> [LARRY BOWA]

"I'm glad to see Bobby make the All-Star team and finally get some of the recognition he's earned," Larry Bowa comments. "Bobby has all the tools. He runs, hits, has a good arm, and has power. He doesn't do things spectacularly but he gets the job done every day."

Bob Kelly Abreu was born in Venezuela. The Astros inked him as a non-drafted free agent at the age of sixteen. He spent four complete seasons in the Astros' minor-league system before first being called up to the parent club in 1996. Bobby found himself in right field on opening day in Houston the following

spring. Unfortunately, he injured the hamate bone in his right hand and languished on the disabled list for more than a month. After a few minor-league rehabs, Bobby was recalled by the Astros. He responded by hitting .306 for the remainder of the season.

On the heels of that performance, Houston surprisingly made Abreu available in the expansion draft. Tampa Bay snatched him up as their third overall pick on November 18. That very same day, the Phils swapped Kevin Stocker for him. The next spring, Bobby was in right field for the Phils on opening day. He turned in a stellar season. He was a model of consistency. His average stayed above .300 all season long. He finished with a .312 batting average and .409 OBP. He led the Phils in both categories. His .427 average with runners in scoring position was tops in the majors.

Abreu outdid his '97 performance the next season. His .335 average was third best in the NL, and the highest Phillie batting average since Tony Gonzalez hit .339 in 1967. Abreu's .446 OBP was third highest in the NL and the highest Phillie mark since Richie Ashburn's .449 in 1955.

After hitting .316 in the 2000 campaign, in 2001 Bobby became the only Phillie ever (and the 25th in major league history) to slam 30 homers and swipe 30 stolen bases in the same year. He reprised the feat in 2004.

In 2002, Abreu led the NL in doubles. He was only the third Phillie in history to stroke 50 doubles in a single season (Hall of Famers Chuck Klein—1930 and 1932—and Ed Delahanty in 1899 were the others). In 2003, Bobby walked a hundred times for the fifth straight season, becoming the first Phillie to do so since Roy Thomas strung six consecutive 100-walk seasons together between 1899 and 1904. Going into 2005, Bobby has now walked a 100 times for six consecutive seasons. Only Mike Schmidt and Roy Thomas had more 100-walk seasons. Each had seven. Abreu seems a cinch to claim that Phillie record as well.

Abreu's feats and figures on the diamond are impressive. With his 2004 All-Star selection, the guy is finally seen as a big fish in the big major league pond. Curt Schilling is one of Abreu's peers who admires his talent. "I give the guy immense praise," Schilling offers. "Bobby has talent, but he takes it beyond that. He's smart. He plays the game intelligently and he really studies pitchers."

Abreu has a human side as well. For Phillie fans who might wonder why he points upward after a home run, Bobby is not mimicking the gesture *du jour*.

"I do that for my father," Abreu reveals. "My father was good to me all my life. He's not alive now to see me. Every time I cross the plate, I dedicate it to him, to his memory."

Bobby has been quietly involving himself in the Delaware Valley community as well. Despite the fact that he returns annually to his native Venezuela to play winter baseball, Bobby lends his name and fame to some worthwhile Philly-area charities. In 2003, he purchased $10,000 worth of tickets to every Friday home game for kids in his "Abreu's Amigos" program. He was also the Honorary Chairman for the American Red Cross Blood Drive in 2001.

Above: Bobby Abreu has 166 career round-trippers heading into the 2005 season.
Jonathan Daniel/Getty Images

DICK ALLEN

It's not often that a rookie almost carries his team to a pennant. Richie Allen (with equivalent support from Johnny Callison) almost led the Phils to a pennant in 1964. Incidentally, a few years after '64, Richie let it be known that he preferred to be called Dick Allen. He didn't like the name Richie. Dick Allen didn't like a lot of things in the baseball world of the early sixties.

"I took Dick over to a school in Germantown where I was showing *Chasing the Dream*, my documentary on Hank Aaron," Mike Tollin, Hollywood producer and Philly native relates. Mike also produced *ARLI$$* and the movie *Radio*. "I introduced Dick Allen to the school kids. I touted all his great accomplishments—Rookie of the Year, MVP, etc. The kids didn't know who Dick Allen was, so my intro didn't connect too well with them. During the show, I glanced over and Dick had vanished. I went outside and saw him standing there. He told me the movie was just too painful to watch. He didn't want to dredge up all those memories—what he and other African Americans had to endure in those days."

Growing up in tiny Wampum, Pennsylvania, Dick Allen became a high school superstar. He was an All-America basketball player and a highly recruited baseball player.

Left: Dick Allen batted .300 in each of his first four seasons in Philadelphia, and represented the Phils in three All-Star Games.
Courtesy of the Philadelphia Phillies

Born: March 8, 1942, Wampum, Pennsylvania
Positions: First Base, Third Base, Left Field
Years with the Phillies: 1964-1969, 1975-1976
Uniform Number: 15
Major League Stats: .292, 351 HR, 1,119 RBI
Phillies Postseason Stats: 1976 NLCS: .222, 0 HR, 0 RBI
Honors:
• 1964 National League Rookie of the Year
• 1972 American League MVP
• National League All Star 1965, 1966, 1967, 1970
• AL All-Star 1972, 1973 (injured), 1974

Maje McDonnell, ex-Phils coach and scout, recalls: "John Ogden, our Phillies scout, practically lived with Dick Allen when Dick was in high school. Scouts had to be salesmen in those days. That was before the draft. John was a good salesman but he was more. He was like a father to Dick. Dick trusted John. That's why he signed with the Phils. After he signed, he had it rough. He left Wampum to play in Little Rock, Arkansas in the Deep South. Little Rock was a really tough city for blacks back then. Dick was still a teenager when he was playing there. He had to handle a lot of hurtful things—things he wasn't used to, like not being able to stay in hotels, riding in the back of buses, and being prohibited from white-only restrooms."

Dick Allen was a fabled athlete. His exploits and potential in high school sparked enormous national interest. He received basketball scholarship offers from schools all over the country. All the major league baseball teams were courting him. He finally chose baseball and signed for a hefty bonus.

"I grew up in central Pennsylvania," Phils' VP Larry Shenk says. "I remember watching Dick play basketball in the Pennsylvania high school championships at Hershey. He was the point guard for Wampum. They ran a controlled offense in those days. That restricted Dick. The guy could leap 18 inches over the rim from a standing jump. He could dribble, shoot, the whole package. There's no telling what he would have done if he

"He hit one into the lights in center field in Tampa. I'll never forget that shot."

[LARRY SHENK]

had been freed up to play a wide-open game like they do today."

When Dick arrived in Philadelphia in 1964, the whole city was excited. He had wowed everyone in spring training.

Larry Shenk reconstructs the scene: "I figure Dick must have hit 15 homers in '64 spring training. We didn't keep track of those things back then. He hit one into the lights in center field in Tampa. I'll never forget that shot.

"The fans were expecting a lot from him when he came up. I'll tell you this much—Dick didn't have anything handed over to him as a rookie. When he reported to spring training, Don Hoak was not about to relinquish his regular third base spot to Dick Allen. Hoak was a gruff guy, an ex-Marine nicknamed Tiger. He was the starting third baseman for the '60 Pirates' championship team. During infield

practice, Hoak positioned himself behind Dick. Hoak stood there glowering, arms folded. Of course Dick did take Hoak's job away."

Dick Allen went on to do great things as a Phil. He batted .318 in his rookie year. He hit 29 homers, drove in 92, and scored 125 runs. In fact, Dick batted at least .300 in each of his first four seasons. Aside from 1964, he led the Phils in total bases every year between 1964 and 1969. He made the All-Star team three times as a Phillie third baseman—twice as a starter. When he moved to left field in 1968, his average dipped to .263 (which embarrassingly was *second* highest on the eighth-place Phils behind Tony Gonzalez' .264). Allen slugged 33 homers and knocked in 90 runs that year.

Dick Allen always managed to keep Larry Shenk, the Phils PR guru, busy. Shenk handled more than his share of Dick Allen peccadilloes.

"Dick made life exciting for me," Shenk recalled. "He showed up late for team buses, team meetings, and the like more than a few times. Once Dick missed a flight to St. Louis. I was listening to the radio on my way home after a long week. I had to rush back to the office immediately to deal with the media situation. And that incident wasn't the only one.

"I was in a movie theater when I was called away the time Dick cut his hand on a headlight. In those days, the media was print. That was virtually it. There were no live TV conferences, no ESPNs, etc. Media meant the *Bulletin*, the *Inquirer* and the *Daily News*. They were our primary points of contact and communication. Anyway, I went to the hospital where Dick was being treated. The doctor showed me where Dick's hand had been cut. Then I showed the reporters. I diagrammed on my hand where Dick had been cut. The newspapers printed a photo of my hand in their papers the next day to show where Dick Allen had been injured."

Dick changed positions again in 1969, this time to first base. The "Wampum Walloper" upped his average to .288 that year. He also slammed 32 homers. However, he never found peace with the boos and catcalls he heard from Philly fans. He took to scrawling words with his spikes in the dirt around first base. He printed words like "boo." The next year he was shuffled off to the Cardinals where he spent one season. He spent another lone season in LA before trekking to Chicago. With the White Sox in 1972, he enjoyed his finest season. Dick won the MVP that year. He hit .308. His 37 home runs and 113 RBIs topped the American League.

Dick's feats that season kindled some Windy City legends. Two of his 37 home runs, for instance, came on July 31, 1972, in Comiskey Park. Each round-tripper was socked off Bert Blyleven. Each ball traveled so fast that it dipped precipitously in front of centerfielder Bobby Darwin before skittering unencumbered into another zip code in the deepest part of the park. He followed up on his MVP season with two more .300-plus campaigns in Chicago. Shockingly he then returned to Philly.

"Paul Owens called me in his office one day," Larry Shenk recalls. "He asked me, 'What would happen if we bought Dick Allen back?' I told him I thought the fans wouldn't accept him. I was wrong. The fans loved Dick Allen the second time around."

Dick Allen played first base in 1975 and 1976. He batted .233 and .268, respectively. He did manage to wallop 15 homers in only 298 at bats in '76. Most importantly, for a young club, Dick Allen was a legend and a positive presence in the clubhouse.

"I remember Dick as a guy who laughed and joked a lot," Larry Christensen recalls. "I'll tell you a funny one. He really helped my hitting—indirectly. I hit with a big bat—36" in length and 36 ounces in weight. One day I broke my own bat and didn't have another one. Crash's bat was the only other big bat in the clubhouse, so I borrowed it. It weighed 42 ounces. I ended up hitting two homers off Mickey Lolich. Then Crash made me give it back to him."

Crash was a nickname that Philly sportswriters hung on Dick Allen. In fact, *Crash* is the title of Dick Allen's biography, written with Tim Whitaker, a former Germantown *Courier* staff writer.

After 1976, Dick played only one more season. He went to Oakland and quietly finished out his career.

"Dick came back for the Final Innings ceremonies when we closed the Vet," Larry Shenk reports. "I still hear from him or hear about him when I least expect it. I got a call from a barber near Kennett Square a little while ago. The guy said, 'I had an unexpected visitor today—Dick Allen.' Dick was in the area because he had gone to Tug McGraw's funeral. Dick remembered that John Ogden, the scout who signed him, was buried somewhere near Kennett Square. Dick figured the town barber would be the guy most likely to know which cemetery."

"Dick was a very sensitive man and tough to read for a lot of people," Larry Shenk sums up. "He always called me 'Daddy,' for reasons unknown. Still does. Dick loved his mother, loved his privacy, and loved his horses!"

One-time Phil and popular sport personality Bob Uecker attests to Allen's love of horses. Uecker concludes, "I'll never forget the time I was staying in the Presidential Arms on City Line Avenue. I got a call from Dick who told me, 'I'm sitting here at the bar. Come on down and see how I got here.' I had no idea what he was driving at. So I went down. There was Dick sitting at the bar. And over in the corner of the bar, I saw a horse. Dick had ridden the horse from Germantown to City Line Avenue."

RICHIE ASHBURN

"Hard to believe Harry ..."

From 1971 to 1997, Phillie broadcaster Richie Ashburn drummed those words into Philly sportalk. Ashburn uttered them during frustrating Phillies moments (so he said them as frequently as a frustrated parent says, "Clean up your room") to his partner in the booth, Harry Kalas.

Rough, tough Philadelphia fell in love with Richie's understated Midwest sense of humor and homespun observations. Richie grew up in Tilden, Nebraska, far away from Philly's Connie Mack Stadium where he forged a Hall of Fame career (Nebraska has been fertile ground for Philly. Fellow Phillies Hall of Famer Grover Cleveland Alexander was also a Cornhusker). Richie Ashburn was an adopted Philadelphian, perhaps the Quaker City's most beloved immigrant since Connie Mack headed south from Boston.

Old-timers in Philly remember Richie Ashburn as the fleet center fielder who tracked down everything that fell from the sky at 21st and Lehigh, site of Connie Mack Stadium. Ashburn had plenty of room to roam in his home park. The centerfield fence was a distant 447 feet away from

Born: March 19, 1927, Tilden, Nebraska
Died: September 9, 1997, New York, NY
Position: Center Field
Years with the Phillies: 1948-1959
Uniform Number: 1
Major League Stats: .308, 29 HR, 586 RBI
Phillies Postseason Stats: 1950 World Series .176, 0 HR, 0 RBI
Honors:
• 1948 *The Sporting News* Rookie of the Year
• Selected to five All-Star teams and started as a rookie in 1948
• Phillies retired his uniform number 1 on September 24, 1979
• Elected to the Hall of Fame by the Veterans Committee in 1995
• Chosen for the Phils All-Centennial team in 1983
• In 1998, the Phils established the Richie Ashburn Special Achievement Award given annually to the member of the Phillies organization who has demonstrated the same loyalty, dedication and passion for the game as the award's namesake.

Left: Hall of Famer Richie Ashburn led the National League in hits three times and batting average three times in the 1950s. Ashburn served as the Phillies' broadcaster from 1971 through his death in 1997. *Courtesy of the Philadelphia Phillies*

> # "I was fortunate as a pitcher. I had terrific defensive players behind me. Eddie Waitkus was as smooth as they come at first base. Granny could play any position in the infield and do the job. Puddin' Head Jones was a fine third baseman. Even Del Ennis was better than given people gave him credit for. But the best of all was Richie. I can't tell you how many games he won with his glove and speed."
>
> [ROBIN ROBERTS—PHILLIES HALL OF FAME PITCHER]

home plate. Byrum Saam, the Phillies original Hall of Fame announcer (Saam preceded Harry Kalas into Cooperstown) popularized, "And Putt Putt puts it away." Putt Putt was Richie's nickname because of the way he motored after fly balls.

Putt Putt really did put them away, plenty of them. In the heyday—the "Say Hey" day of Willie, Mickey, and the Duke—Richie put more fly balls away than any of his contemporaries. Whitey Ashburn led the league a record-setting nine times in number of chances handled. Four times he surpassed 500 putouts in a season—the only major leaguer ever to do so. Nine times he eclipsed the 400-putout mark, which is another Ashburn exclusive.

MAJE McDONNELL: "Richie could run them down as well as anyone I've ever seen out there. Eddie Sawyer used to tell Del Ennis, 'Just let Richie take anything he can get to.' That's what Richie did. He covered the whole outfield. Funny thing—for a couple of years [1955 and 1956], we had a guy playing right field named Jim Greengrass. The joke in Philly those years was: 'What covers the whole outfield?' Everyone expected Ashburn to be the answer, but it was 'Green grass, like Greengrass.' I guess that joke wouldn't have worked at the Vet."

ROBIN ROBERTS: "I was fortunate as a pitcher. I had terrific defensive players behind me. Eddie Waitkus was as smooth as they come at first base. Granny could play any position in the infield and do the job. Puddin' Head Jones was a fine third baseman. Even Del Ennis was better than people gave him credit for. But the best of all was Richie. I can't tell you how many games he won with his glove and speed."

Richie Ashburn came up as a catcher. Eddie Sawyer converted him to an outfielder to profit from his speed. Ashburn's transition was splendid.

Above: Richie Ashburn was elected to the National Baseball Hall of Fame in 1995. He was inducted alongside fellow Phillies legend Mike Schmidt. *Rich Pilling/MLB/Getty Images*

He became one of the finest outfielders of his time. Gaining recognition, as such, was an arduous process. Richie's peers were a daunting bunch. Besides Mays, Mantle, and Snider, there was a battalion of other fine centerfielders in the '50s. Early in the decade, the Pirates had Frank Thomas in center. Bill Virdon—or "The Quail" as he was known—took over later on. Virdon also played center for the Cards. The Cards boasted Wally Moon and later Curt Flood in center. In fact, Stan Musial was the Cards' center fielder in 1952, and 1964 MVP Ken Boyer in 1957. The Reds had Gus Bell and the Braves had the fleet Billy Bruton.

Besides that formidable slate of peers, Richie Ashburn's celebrity also suffered because he wasn't a power hitter. Whitey hit only 29 career home runs. However, Ashburn led the league in hits three times. Three times he led in batting average. Four times he led in walks. Most impressive of all, he led the Senior Circuit in on base percentage four times.

The Ashburn name is plastered all over the Phillies all-time record book. He played more games (1,794), slapped out more hits (2,217), wheedled more walks (946), and stepped up to the plate (7,122 at bats) more times than any Phillie except for Mike Schmidt. Ashburn leads the franchise in singles with 1,811, ranks sixth in doubles with 287, and fourth in triples with 97. His 199 stolen bases slide him into fifth place on the Phils' all-time list.

Richie's .311 lifetime Phillie batting average places him eighth all time, while his .394 on-base

> ## "He could drive a pitcher crazy. He'd just set up shop at home plate and foul off one pitch after another."
>
> [BUBBA CHURCH—FORMER PHILLIES TEAMMATE]

percentage ranks third behind leader Bobby Abreu (.414) and runner-up John Kruk (.400).

Despite his impressive accomplishments, home run hitters, as the expression goes, drive Cadillacs. Singles hitters do not. Whitey always told a funny story about negotiating his salary with Phillies GM John Quinn the year after Whitey had won the batting title.

"They offered me a reduction in salary," Richie said. "I told Quinn, 'But I *won the batting title!*' Quinn countered, 'But you didn't hit them far enough. They were all singles.' I told him, 'If I had hit them any farther, they would have been outs.'"

Arguably, Richie Ashburn is Philadelphia's most beloved athlete. He was the kind of all-out competitor that the Quaker City loves. His uniform was permanently dirt and grass stained. He played the game the old-fashioned way. He was heads up at all times, looking for every subtle edge.

Whitey spoke to Little League baseball teams often during his time in Philadelphia. He passed on a lot of practical tips. In those days, the basebags were strapped rather than pinned in place. Richie suggested kicking the bag as far as possible toward second whenever you reached first base. That gives you an inch or more advantage on pick-off attempts and an inch or two jump toward second for a steal. Whitey practiced what he preached. On a few occasions he avoided an out because he had repositioned the bag.

LIVE TO SEE ANOTHER DAY

Richie often said that a single season with the Mets was enough. He had turned 35 on March 19, 1962. He felt that each additional season with the Mets threatened to remove multiple years from his life. So he retired. Richie's sentiments were not unprecedented. Former Whiz Kids skipper Eddie Sawyer managed the Phils from 1948-1952. He left the managing profession at that point. Eddie worked in the Philadelphia area as a salesman in private industry. He resurfaced in baseball in 1958 to manage the Phils once again. Under Sawyer, the Phils were buried in last place in 1958 and 1959. The 1960 team offered even less promise. So Sawyer bolted. He jolted Philly when he resigned unexpectedly after the opening game in 1960. The skipper explained to the Philly press, "I'm 49. I want to live to be 50."

In a nutshell, Philadelphia loved Richie Ashburn. He was the David whose guile and grit zonked the Goliaths. He was one of the sport's last great bunters and perhaps as crafty at "working a pitcher" as anyone who ever played.

Bubba Church (a Whiz Kids teammate of Whitey's who has since passed away) once described how Ashburn shook up their former Phillie teammate, Russ "Mad Monk" Meyer, after Meyer had been traded to Brooklyn.

BUBBA CHURCH: "Richie came up with the bases full. He could drive a pitcher crazy. He'd just set up shop at home plate and foul off one pitch after another. Russ wasn't known for his patience. When Richie fouled off about ten straight pitches, the Mad Monk just plunked Richie in the middle of his back. Meyer did it on purpose out of sheer frustration. He forced a run home. The Monk told me later, 'He just got me so mad I had to hit him. We were ahead, so the run didn't matter. We won anyway.'"

After winning his second and final batting title in 1958, Richie slumped to .266 in 1959. The Phils dealt him to the Cubs in 1960. He rallied at Wrigley, hitting a respectable .291 and leading the league in walks with 116. When his average trailed off to .257 in 1961, however, the Cubs placed his name in the expansion draft. The brand-new New York Mets gobbled Richie up and Putt Putt came through. Richie led the Mets, the worst team in major-league history, with a .306 batting average. Richie apparently likened that honor to being selected valedictorian of the summer school class. He retired after that woeful year at age 35.

When Richie retired, he was a scant 427 hits short of 3,000. He immediately accepted a job as a Phillies broadcaster and remained at the post until his death on September 9, 1997.

Richie Ashburn left his mark all over his adopted city. The main concourse at Citizens Bank Park is Ashburn Alley. The city dedicated a ballpark near the stadium complex in South Philly as Richie Ashburn Park. One of the fields in the Carpenter Complex in Clearwater Florida is named Ashburn Field. In 1998, the Phillies created the Richie Ashburn Special Achievement Award, which is presented annually to the member of the Phillies organization who demonstrates the "same loyalty, dedication and passion for the game as the award's namesake."

Richie Ashburn accomplished all those things, yet it took a targeted effort and several years of tense anticipation before Richie Ashburn was finally inducted into the Hall of Fame. Hard to believe, Harry.

STEVE BEDROSIAN

The Phillies "owned" the Cy Young Award in the '80s. Steve Carlton won Cy Young Awards in 1980 and 1982. John Denny won one in 1983. And Steve Bedrosian—or "Bedrock" as he was nicknamed—won in 1987.

Bedrock was carrying on a fine Phils bullpen tradition. Jim Konstanty was the first reliever in baseball history to win a major award. Working almost exclusively out of the bullpen, Konstanty won the MVP Award in 1950. After Konstanty, the Phils boasted a succession of good '50s-'60s relievers, like Jack Meyer, Jack Baldschun, and Turk Farrell. The tradition continued through the '70s, '80s, and into the '90s.

Strong as that tradition is, other than Bedrock, no Phillie reliever ever won a Cy Young Award. Steve Bedrosian, however, is remembered as one of the team's true "characters."

"Bedrock has to be one of the craziest guys ever to hit this clubhouse," Video Dan Stephenson recalls. "He used to play a game—I guess you'd call it a game—that he called 'mad ball.' Don't ask me where that name came from. And don't ask why he did it. I have no idea. Bedrock would burst into the video room with a bat and ball and yell 'Mad ball!'

Born: December 6, 1957, Methuen, Mass.
Position: Relief Pitcher
Years with the Phillies: 1986-1989
Uniform Number: 40
Major League Stats: 76-79, 3.38 ERA, 184 saves
Honors:
• 1987 NL Cy Young Award
• 1987 NL Fireman of the Year
• 1987 Rolaids Relief Man Award
• 1987 Baseball America NL Pitcher of the Year
• 1987 Phillie NL All-Star

He'd swing the bat and slam the ball into the room. The ball would hit the wall and ricochet everywhere. It was a riot to watch the new guys—the guys who had no idea what 'mad ball' meant. When Bedrock yelled 'Mad ball,' every veteran would duck for cover. The new guys would wonder why. Next thing they knew, they'd be dodging the ball banging around the room and wondering if everyone in the majors was crazy."

Bedrock sported a relief pitcher's mentality and personality. He introduced the angel-wing on the pitching mound to the sport. At the closing ceremonies at the Vet in September 2003, Bedrock delighted the nostalgic throng by reenacting his angel wing shtick on the mound.

Left: Steve Bedrosian took home the Phillies' fourth Cy Young Award of the 1980s in 1987, following a season in which he recorded 40 saves and a 2.83 ERA.
Courtesy of the Philadelphia Phillies

"I heard this godawful pounding on my door. Turns out it was Bedrock. He had gotten an axe and started smashing the door down. When he got it part way open, he stuck his head in like Jack Nicholson in The Shining, and said, 'Heeeere's Johnny' "

[DAN STEPHENSON—PHILLIES VIDEO DIRECTOR]

"Bedrock was a fun guy," Milt Thompson remembers. "He was a lively guy around the clubhouse and a great competitor on the mound."

"Bedrock marched to his own drummer," Harry Kalas recalls. "He had that Boston accent and was forever clowning around until he took the mound. He loved his Boston sport teams and was a rabid fan of all the sports."

Bedrock came to the Phils in 1986 by way of Atlanta. From his rookie season in 1981 to 1985, Steve was mainly a reliever. He appeared in 189 games in that period and started only nine of them. In 1985, the Braves decided to bust Bedrock out of the pen. He started 37 games that season. His record tumbled to 7-15. In the off season, the Braves shipped him to the Phils, where Bedrock returned to the bullpen forevermore. Till his retirement in 1995, he never started another major-league game.

Bedrock had some good years with the Braves. In '82 his ERA glittered at 2.42 and he ranked 15th in the senior circuit in saves. He climbed to number eight in '83. His 1984 ERA of 2.37 placed him fourth in the NL among pitchers who tossed at least 80 innings (the Phils' Larry Andersen was fifth on that same list).

In his first season in the Quaker City, Bedrosian recorded 29 saves, fifth best in the NL.

He followed with 40 saves in 1987, which was the best in baseball and a Phillies club record. At that time, only four men in the game's history (Dave Righetti, Bruce Sutter, Dan Quisenberry, and Jeff Reardon) had topped Bedrosian's one-year save total. For his efforts, Bedrock was awarded the Cy Young Award, the NL Fireman of the Year Award and the Rolaids Relief Man Award as the top reliever in all of professional baseball. Bedrock was 5-3 in 65 appearances. His 2.83 ERA ranked seventh in the NL. All the while, he was shaping a reputation in Philly as a wild and crazy guy off the mound.

"At one point, Lee Elia declared the video room off limits during the game," Dan Stephenson chuckles. "Too many guys were walking down the runway and hanging out there while the game was going on. Lee gave me strict orders not to let anyone in. Well, Bedrock was the team's closer. He made a habit of hanging in the video room till about the sixth or seventh. Then he'd head down to the bullpen. After Elia spoke to me, I locked the door to the video room. Along comes Bedrock, knocking at my door, demanding me to let him in. I told him I couldn't. I refused to open the door and Bedrock walked away. A few minutes later, I heard this godawful pounding on my door. Turns out it was Bedrock. He had gotten an axe and started smashing the door down. When he got it part way open, he stuck his head in like Jack Nicholson in *The Shining*, and said, "Heeeere's Johnny!"

Bedrock followed his Cy Young season with a 6-6 record and 28 saves. His ERA mushroomed to 3.75. The '88 Phils were swooning from the departure of Mike Schmidt. In '87, the Phils finished 80-82 in the tough NL East. In the wake of Schmidt's retirement, they tumbled to 65-95—35.5 games behind the division-leading Mets. Save opportunities became rare.

Bedrosian played a partial year for the Phils in 1989, going 2-3 with six saves. In mid season, he was dealt to the Giants, the eventual division-winners who were in need of a closer. His record with San Francisco was 1-4. He boasted 23 saves with San Francisco, however, giving him a season total of 29, good for ninth place on the NL save list. His final year as a closer came in 1990 as a Giant. Bedrock saved 17 that season and posted a 9-9 record as the Giants slipped to third place.

In 1991, San Francisco replaced Bedrock with Dave Righetti as their closer. Steve was shipped to Minnesota. He spent a year there before returning to Atlanta. His final productive season came in 1993 as a Brave. Bedrock was 5-2 that year with a nifty 1.63 ERA. His adjusted ERA was an over-the-top 2.46. However he didn't get the opportunity to face his old mates, the Phils, in the 1993 National League Championship Series.

Steve Bedrosian played sparingly the next two seasons for Atlanta before retiring after 1995.

"Bedrock kept things interesting wherever he was," Dan Stephenson sums up. "We did find a way to keep him quiet, though. He loved the Three Stooges. He knew their routines backward and forward. If you put an old Stooges tape on, Bedrock could fill in all the dialogue for you, word for word. I used to keep Stooges tapes around, just so he wouldn't play mad ball."

Below: Steve Bedrosian saved games for the Phillies from 1986 through 1989.
Courtesy of the Philadelphia Phillies

JOHNNY CALLISON

Predictions for superstardom tend to be an albatross. Baseball experts expected big things from Johnny Callison when he broke into baseball. Callison had the tools. He could hit, hit with power, run, throw, and field. Unfortunately, he played in an era chock full of great outfielders like Hank Aaron, Willie Mays, Mickey Mantle, Frank Robinson, and Roberto Clemente. That crew outshined outfielders who were mere stars—ordinary stars—like John Callison. Even eventual Hall of Famer Al Kaline was eclipsed.

Nonetheless, when Callison's moment to shine came, he didn't miss it. Johnny Callison entered the 1964 All-Star game in New York as a replacement for Henry Aaron. The National League trailed 4-3 in the bottom of the ninth. Willie Mays started the inning off by walking after fouling off five straight third strikes. Willie stole second before scoring the tying run on a single to short right. One intentional walk and two outs later, Johnny Callison stepped to the plate. He was facing Dick Radatz, a 6-6, 230-pound flamethrowing AL reliever known as "The Monster." Radatz owned the top strikeout/innings pitched ratio (1.13) in all of baseball from 1960-1965—besting even the legendary Sandy Koufax (1.07).

Born: March 12, 1939, Qualis, Oklahoma
Position: Outfield
Years with the Phillies: 1960-1969
Uniform Number: 6
Major League Stats: .264, 226 HR, 840 RBI
Honors:
- NL Phillie All-Star 1962 1964, 1965
- 1964 All-Star game MVP
- NL leader in doubles (1966)
- NL leader in triples (1962, 1965)

Callison walloped the first pitch high into the Shea Stadium night. It landed in the right field seats for a walk-off home run—the second in All-Star game history (Stan Musial hit the other—a round-tripper off Frank Sullivan's first pitch in the 12th inning of the '55 game).

John Callison should not be remembered for that feat alone. He enjoyed a fine career. Johnny was the leader and biggest star on the Phillies in the early '60s.

"If John had only weighed about 25 pounds more," Clay Dalrymple, ex-Phils' catcher suggests, "There's no telling how great he could have been. He was not a big guy, but he had terrific power for his size. He had all the tools. He also had the ability to carry a club. Johnny *did* carry us a number of times in '64."

Left: Johnny Callison was one of baseball's unsung stars in the 1960s. He was the Phillies' leader and biggest star for the decade.
Courtesy of the Philadelphia Phillies

Callison and Dalrymple roomed together with the Phils. It was a natural pairing. Both were Californians dealing with the East Coast for the first time.

"We lived about three blocks apart in Glenside," Dalrymple recalls. "We'd ride in to the game together sometimes. Johnny was serious about baseball. He was always trying to improve."

Callison grew up in Bakersfield, California, and signed with the Chicago White Sox organization. He broke in with the Go-Go Sox in their pennant-winning year of 1959.

"We had a good club," Johnny reminisces. "Luis Aparicio, Norm Cash, Nellie Fox, Ted

"I had a good year personally. I gained a lot of respect because of my homer in the All-Star game. I finished second in the MVP voting. But it was hard to live through the end of that season. It seemed that we couldn't come out on top no matter what we did."

Callison did his best to turn around the team's tailspin. How often does a player hit three homers in a losing cause? That's what Callison did when he launched three dingers out of Connie Mack Stadium on September 27, 1964. The Phils lost the game 12-7. Effectively, that loss was the team's swan song.

Callison clouted 32 homers, his pinnacle, in 1964. He would never again hit 20. His performance

"If John had only weighed about 25 pounds more, there's no telling how great he could have been. He was not a big guy, but he had terrific power for his size."

[CLAY DALRYMPLE—PHILLIES TEAMMATE]

Kluszewski, Early Wynn, and others. I was happy in Chicago. I wanted to stay. But I played winter ball that year in Venezuela. I hurt my knee and Chicago traded me to the Phillies. Philadelphia was the last place I wanted to go!

"At first, I wasn't real happy in Philly. Gene Mauch platooned me till '62. But things got better."

When he became a full-time performer, Johnny responded by batting .300 and socking 23 round-trippers. His previous high in homers had been nine. The next year, he jacked his homer total up to 26 and hit .284.

Then came 1964, a bittersweet year for Philadelphia and the Phillies. Perhaps it was more bittersweet for Johnny Callison than anyone.

"The memories of that season were the best memories I have of baseball," Callison reflects today.

started a slow decline in 1965. So did the team. The Phils managed to stay on the right side of .500 in 1965 and again in 1966. However by the end of the decade, they played at an awful .389 clip.

Johnny hit .265 with 16 homers and 64 RBIs for that squad in 1969.

"I was hurting the last five years of my career," Johnny admits. "I had to tape my knee every day. I had a pinched nerve in my right arm. It was painful to play."

It was painful for the Phils to deal the popular Callison away. However, in 1970, Johnny was shipped to the Cubs.

"I actually played pretty well in Chicago," Johnny says. "I hit 19 homers [the most he had hit since 1964] and batted .264 my first season. But I didn't see eye to eye with manager Leo Durocher.

He platooned me. It was tough to go back to being platooned. It's tough to get your rhythm and stroke when you don't play every day, especially when you're used to it."

In 1971, John was limited to 290 at bats with the Cubs. His average sank to .210 and he was dealt to the Yankees in the off season. John hit 10 homers over the next two seasons as a Bronx Bomber.

"I liked New York," Callison admits. "Ralph Houk was good to me. He was a good manager. But I couldn't run anymore. I was in too much pain. It was time to get out."

Johnny's name still shows up in the Phils' all-time record book. He's one of only two Phils who can claim two three-home run games. Mike Schmidt is the other. Ten times Callison hit two homers in a game. Only nine other Phils have done it more. He strung together four consecutive 20-homer seasons. Only five other Phillies can claim more. He also hit five walk-off homers for the Phils—more than any other Philllie other than Mike Schmidt and Cy Williams. And John Callison remains the only Phil ever to win an All-Star Game MVP.

John remained in the Delaware Valley area—the rare Californian who turns Pennsylvanian.

"I bought a house here in 1965," John confides. "My kids were growing up in the area. I didn't want them to have to relocate so we stayed. The Delaware Valley's a nice area. And the people in Philly have always been great. So yes, I guess I am a converted Philadelphian. I won't be going anywhere else at this point. That's for sure."

Below: Johnny Callison's homer off of Dick Radatz in the bottom of the ninth won the 1964 All-Star Game for the National League.
Courtesy of the Philadelphia Phillies

STEVE CARLTON

S teve Carlton epitomized his nickname "Lefty" for many of his fans. Lefty was as enigmatic to the public as he was baffling to opposing batsmen. Carlton declared a standoff with the Philadelphia media early in his Phillies career. He didn't talk to the press. His stoic mound mien made him appear all the more sullen. His teammates and friends, however, feel those behaviors skewed his image. Nonetheless, legions of fans lionized Carlton. They interpreted his actions as being principled, single-minded, and strong.

Video Dan Stephenson, head of the Philadelphia Phillies video department, was a good friend and confidant of Steve Carlton. Dan says the public never really got to see the real Lefty.

"Lefty was one of the best loved guys ever in the clubhouse," Dan recalls. "He didn't talk to reporters, which was misleading. His teammates thought the world of him."

Lefty does and did hold some unconventional notions. That goes with being left-handed, according to old-time baseball wisdom. Baseball players tend to be a beer-and-bar-crawl crowd. Lefty in contrast was a wine aficionado. He pursues that same passion now that he's retired.

Born: December 22, 1944, Miami, Florida
Position: Pitcher
Years with the Phillies: 1972-1986
Uniform Number: 32
Major League Stats: 329-244, 3.22 ERA
Phillies Postseason Stats: NLCS (1976, 1977, 1978, 1980, 1983) and 1981 Divisional Playoffs: 4-4, 3.59; World Series (1980, 1983): 2-1, 2.49 ERA
Honors:
• First pitcher to win four Cy Young Awards (1972, 1977, 1980, 1982)
• Elected to Hall of Fame 1994
• Phillie uniform number 32 retired on July 29, 1989
• NL Pitcher of the Year, 1972, 1977, 1980, 1982
• NL Pitcher of the Week 1977, 1980
• Starting LHP on Phillies All-Centennial Team
• Starting LHP on All-Vet Team

Left: Steve Carlton won four Cy Young Awards for the Phillies in the 1970s and '80s. He is considered the top left-hander of his generation.
Manny Millan/Icon SMI

Carlton continues to shy away from the limelight these days. In his playing years, besides keeping a low profile, Carlton devoted himself to a special training regiment. He adopted a singular, relentless approach to conditioning—an approach that was foreign and inscrutable to the sport's old guard.

"Lefty chose not to exercise with the rest of the team," Dan points out. "He developed his own workouts. He befriended Gus Hoefling, Roman Gabriel's personal trainer. Gabriel was the Eagles' quarterback in the mid-seventies. Roman came from Los Angeles where he quarterbacked the LA Rams. Gabriel had met Gus when they were both on the West Coast. Hoefling had a gym at Venice Beach and his approach to conditioning was very different for its time. Gus based his conditioning program on martial arts and the like—things that were way out of the athletic mainstream in that era.

"For instance, Gus made Lefty push his hand through a rice-filled barrel until he touched the bottom. I used to try to do it myself. You can't believe couldn't believe it. The rice barrel was just one of the unconventional things Lefty used. He put himself through the most rigorous program I've ever seen."

The program paid dividends. Carlton owns one of the sport's glitziest pitching records. He won 329 games with a career ERA of 3.22. His first season as a Phil in 1972 remains one of the greatest seasons any individual ever had. Pitching for the last-place Phils, Carlton tallied 27 victories, which represented a phenomenal 46 percent of his team's wins. His ERA was a sterling 1.97. He won his first Cy Young Award hands down.

"Lefty had the greatest concentration of any pitcher I've seen," Larry Christenson says. "If he lost a game, he focused on the next game immediately. Same thing if he won. He didn't care about anything else except pitching."

> # "Lefty had the greatest concentration of any pitcher I've seen," Larry Christenson says. "If he lost a game, he focused on the next game immediately. Same thing if he won. He didn't care about anything else except pitching."
>
> [LARRY CHRISTENSON—FELLOW PHILLIES PITCHER]

Dan Stephenson adds, "When Lefty cleaned out his locker to go to San Francisco, he was joking and smiling. He hated to leave Philly, but he wasn't upset. He fully believed he could pitch till he was 50 because of the way he conditioned himself. But

how hard it is. Lefty has to be the strongest guy we ever had from the shoulders down to his fingertips. His hand and arm strength along with his leg strength was incredible. When Joe Morgan played here in '83, Joe asked Lefty what he did with the rice barrel. Lefty told him. Joe tried it and couldn't push down much farther than the palm of his hand. Joe was a compact, strong guy too. When Joe gave up, Lefty reached in. I swear he pushed his hand all the way to the bottom in two seconds. Joe Morgan

his arm was wrecked at that point. At the end of his career, a doctor checked out his arm. The guy asked Lefty how many days he had been pitching in pain. Lefty told him about four years! He actually won a Cy Young Award when his arm was killing him.

"Concentration was the key to his success. Johnny Bench hit Carlton well. He used to own Carlton—just like Lefty used to own Dave Parker. It was one of those unexplainable things in baseball. One day, Lefty jumps out 0-2 on Bench who

Above: Steve Carlton threw out the first pitch at the Phillies' new Citizens Bank Park in April 2004.
Jon Adams/Icon SMI

was up there looking for his 2,000th hit. Bench fought off about five nasty pitches. Then he ripped a double. What a phenomenal at-bat and what a phenomenal battle! When Bench was standing on second base, Lefty turned around to him, bowed, and tipped his cap. It was one of those immortal baseball moments where you're thrilled just to be there—two all-time greats battling it out and acknowledging the other's great performance. A few years later, Lefty and I were reminiscing. I reminded Lefty about his tipping his cap to Bench. Lefty had completely forgotten the incident! That was his pitching make-up. He was so locked into pitching that he forgot everything else, even a classic episode like that."

Folk singer Chuck Brodsky—whom the Hall of Fame calls the "Troubadour of Baseball," has written about nine songs on the national pastime (see www.chuckbrodsky.com). Chuck lives in North Carolina now. He's a native Philadelphian and lifelong Phillies fan. The very first baseball song he wrote was called "Lefty". The song talked about a great pitcher who stayed in the game too long. As Brodsky puts it, the composition was "loosely based on Steve Carlton." Lefty did stay in the game a bit too long. He marred his pristine record with some twilight-of-the-career team-trotting.

Lefty broke in as a 20-year-old with the Cardinals in 1965 and turned in some great seasons for the Redbirds. He was the unquestioned ace of the Phils' staff from 1972 (his first year as a Phil) through 1986, when he spent parts of the season with the Phils, the Giants, and the White Sox. He split the 1987 campaign between Cleveland and Minnesota. He reported back to Minnesota in 1988 to pitch nine and two-thirds inglorious innings and close out his career.

Steve Carlton was a shadow of himself during that post-Phillies odyssey. His ERAs with each suc-

cessive team from 1986 until his retirement were 6.18, 5.10, 3.69, 5.37, 6.70, and 16.76.

"Lefty wanted to play so badly," Dan Stephenson continues. "And let me tell you, they loved him in Minnesota! When the Twins won the World Series in '87, I saw the funniest photo. This picture of Kent Hrbek and Kirby Puckett with the president came across my desk. The caption read, "President Reagan congratulates Kent Hrbek and Kirby Puckett for their World Series victory while an unidentified Secret Service Agent looks on. The unidentified agent was Lefty! He was standing behind them in a suit and he was wearing a pair of sunglasses! Lefty didn't suit up for the Series, but the Twins invited him down there to the White House with the team. This reporter obviously didn't recognize Lefty in the shades."

Philadelphia didn't have the opportunity to get acquainted with the fun-loving side of Steve Carlton, the guy who was a cut-up in the clubhouse.

"The first time my future wife, Patti, met Lefty, she thought I said his name was 'Shifty,'" Dan Stephenson chuckles. "Next time she met him, we were all sharing a cab. We straightened her out on 'Shifty's' proper nickname. Then she really got to know him. Lefty will talk your ears off when he's comfortable around you. He loves to talk about his theories on health, government, and life. He was in rare form that night. He was telling Patti that the molecules in the human body are designed to last a thousand years if we take care of ourselves properly. I looked at Lefty, looked at my watch, and said, 'If that's the case, Lefty, you've got about five minutes to go!' It's true that Lefty conditioned himself like a Spartan, but he loved his wine and never missed a good time either. He was one of the greatest ever on the mound. He was also one of the greatest guys ever around the clubhouse. Everyone in the Phillies organization hated to see him go."

Above: Steve Carlton won 27 games in 1972, his first year in Philadelphia. That accounted for a whopping 46 percent of the team's wins.
Courtesy of the Philadelphia Phillies

DAVE CASH

Back in the early '70s, the Pirates were accumulating quality second basemen faster than American televisions networks today are adding schmaltzy reality shows. The '73 Pirates featured Dave Cash and Rennie Stennett. Hall of Famer Bill Mazeroski had just retired in '72 and Cash was his heir apparent. Willie Randolph, who was destined for an esteemed Yankee career, was also waiting in the wings in the minors. The second base-rich Pirates wound up unloading Dave Cash to the Phils.

"It wasn't a popular trade when the Phils got Dave Cash," Phils PR guru Larry Shenk avows. "We traded Ken Brett for him. Brett was a huge fan favorite. He was a nice-looking guy and a pitcher who could hit [Brett hit home runs in a record-setting four consecutive games in June, 1973]. That scores big with the fans. Dave wasn't very well known in Philly at the time of the trade, even though he had some good seasons with the Pirates.

"I didn't know Dave at the time of the trade. I met him on the Phils' Winter Caravan tour. Dave got up to speak at the Holiday Inn on Route 501 in Lancaster and froze at the mic. He didn't know what to say. I remember I felt bad for him at the

Born: June 11, 1948, Utica, New York
Position: Second Base
Years with the Phillies: 1974-1976
Uniform Number: 30
Major League Stats: .283, 21 HR, 426 RBI
Phillies Postseason Stats: 1976 NLCS, .308, 1 RBI
Honors:
• Chosen for NL All-Star team three consecutive years as a Phillie, 1974-1976

time. We kind of saved him. We rushed somebody up there quickly to speak in his place and everything went fine. But my first impression of Dave was that he was quiet or kind of introverted. Was I ever off base! Dave was one of the most vocal guys ever to hit this clubhouse. He became a vocal leader of the club."

Dave Cash was happy to come to Philly.

"They were building a team here in Philly," Dave reflects. "I could see they had a lot of young talent. Pittsburgh had a lot of second basemen. Rennie Stennett and I were splitting time there. So coming to Philly was an opportunity for me to play every day with a young team that was eager."

Left: Dave Cash played only three seasons in Philadelphia—and was named an All-Star each year.
Courtesy of the Philadelphia Phillies

Cash already had a few good seasons under his belt with Pittsburgh when he got to Philly in 1974. He had started spelling Bill Mazeroski at second base in 1970. Maz hit .229 in 367 at bats that year; Cash hit .314 in 210 at bats. The following season,

> ## "As far as inspiring the team, Dave Cash had more positive influence than anyone I ever saw here other than Pete Rose... Dave started that 'Yes we can' thing and we really started to believe in ourselves."
>
> [LARRY CHRISTENSON—PHILLIES TEAMMATE]

Dave eased into the starting second-base slot. He fashioned a .289 batting average in 478 plate appearances. The next year, he hit .282. However in 1973, despite batting only .242, Rennie Stennett had more plate appearances than Dave (Cash batted .271). Following the season, Dave Cash was Philly-bound.

Dave Cash spent only three seasons in the Quaker City. They were the best seasons of his career. He made the All-Star team all three years. He batted over .300 in two out of the three. They were the only .300 seasons (for a full season) he ever had. Most important, Cash played a pivotal role in the Phillies emergence as a baseball power in the seventies.

Prior to his arrival, the Phils had floundered. In 1972, they finished dead last—37 1/2 games behind the front-running Pirates and 11 games behind the next-to-last-place Expos. The '73 Phils improved their record substantially (from 59-97 in 1972 to 71-91 in 1973), but still finished last. They finished a distant six games behind the next-to-last place Cubs. With Cash's arrival in '74, the Phils leaped up to third place. The improvement can't all be pinned on Dave Cash. The promise of Greg Luzinski, Mike Schmidt, and Bob Boone started to be fulfilled. Steve Carlton emerged as one of the game's premier pitchers. Nonetheless as a veteran, Cash instilled a crucial ingredient—confidence. He coined the team's rallying cry, "Yes we can," and the young Phillies finally believed they could.

"I would say that Dave Cash was the sparkplug who built confidence in this organization," Larry Christenson asserts. "He was a vocal guy, always chirping—him and Bowa. But it worked. As far as inspiring the team, Dave Cash had more positive influence than anyone I ever saw here other than Pete Rose. Dave came to Philly when the team wasn't having much success. We had a nucleus but we were young and hadn't yet jelled. Dave started that 'Yes we can' thing and we really started to believe in ourselves."

Cash had played on winners with the Pirates. Other than Steve Carlton, Dave was the only member of the Phils' '74 squad with postseason experience. He stepped up to the role of leader.

"Action Dog," as Cash was known because of his love for the Florida greyhound races, gave the Phillies a more assertive, confident personality.

"Dave was a consistent hitter," Larry Shenk acknowledges. "He had those spindly legs. He kind of looked like a real speed burner but he wasn't. He didn't use speed to get on base. Basically he hit line drives. He hit the ball hard and got lots of hits."

In Cash's three years as a Phillie, only Pete Rose, Rod Carew, and Steve Garvey had more hits in all of baseball. Only Pete Rose, Joe Morgan, and Mike Schmidt in the National League scored more runs than Dave over that same span. And only Ralph Garr, Larry Bowa, and Roger Metzger had more triples.

Dave went to Montreal in 1977 and recorded another good campaign when he batted .289. That season was to be the last full season he would ever bat over .255. He spent a few years with the Expos before retiring in 1980 with San Diego.

"Dave coached for the Phils for awhile," Larry Shenk said. "We've always had good relations with Dave. He did a lot for the club in a short stint. He wound up moving to Clearwater where we have spring training, and he still keeps in touch with us."

Below: Dave Cash came to the Phillies from a championship team in Pittsburgh. That postseason experience was a key ingredient as Cash's new team emerged as a baseball power in the seventies.
Courtesy of the Philadelphia Athletics Historical Society

LARRY CHRISTENSON

Mike Schmidt spent his entire major league career as a Philadelphia Phillie. That's 18 years—the longest major-league career anyone ever had exclusively as a Phillie. The guy who ranks second in that category is a Schmidt contemporary, Larry Christenson, or LC as Philadelphia came to know him.

"There was a reason I never got traded," Larry Christenson jokes. "I was nice to spouses—the wives of Ruly Carpenter, Bill Giles, Paul Owens, and other members of the Phillies brass. I made sure I was polite and courteous to them. That way, the wives would talk their husbands out of trading me."

LC came up with the Phils in 1973. Strangely, the guy who now ranks second in all-time Phillie longevity almost switched uniforms in his very first season. It wasn't a wife who saved him from the trading block though. It was the owner.

"In '73, the Pope [Paul Owens] had already made a deal with Detroit," LC confesses. "Boonie [Bob Boone] and I were supposed to go to the Tigers for Bill Freehan and Jim Northrup. In those days, baseball deals were closed with a handshake. Deals are closed formally now. But the Pope had

Born: November 10, 1953, Everett, Washington
Position: Pitcher
Years with the Phillies: 1973-1983
Uniform Number: 38
Major League Stats: 83-71, 3.79 ERA
Postseason Stats: NLCS (1976, 1977, 1978, 1980) and 1981 Divisional Playoff: 1-1, 5.47; 1980
World Series: 0-1, 108.00 (1/3 of an inning pitched)
Honors:
• NL Player of the Week (1978)
• September 1977, NL Pitcher of the Month
• Ranks twentieth on Phils' all-time list in winning percentage (.53.9%)
• Pitched the Phils centennial game, which was videotaped and placed in a time capsule to be opened one hundred years later.

actually shaken hands on this deal. Ruly Carpenter heard about it the following morning and canceled it."

Carpenter nixed the agreement because he didn't want to lose one of baseball's brightest prospects.

"I made All-American in basketball and baseball in high school," Christenson explains. "I liked basketball more. In high school, I played basketball

Left: Larry Christenson spent his entire 11-year major-league career with the Phillies. The Washington State native was a mainstay in the Phils rotation in the late '70s and early '80s. Courtesy of the Philadelphia Phillies

against Larry Andersen [or LA as he is known]. Larry was a senior. I was a junior. We still joke about the game. Naturally, our team killed his, no matter what LA has to say about it. Anyway, the Phils scout, Bill Harper, watched me pitch back-to-back perfect games. I graduated high school in the Vietnam era when there was a military draft lottery. I was fortunate to draw number 244 in the draft. That was a good number—meaning I wasn't likely to get drafted. That made the coast clear for the Phils to draft me. They did. They drafted me number one in the June '72 baseball draft."

Nothing in LC's previously quiet life in rustic Everett Washington prepared him for what followed after he was drafted.

"The next day, my house was swarming with reporters. It was bedlam," Larry continues. "Later that day, Dallas Green and Brandy Davis of the Phils flew out to my house. I was 19 years old. That night I was sitting in my living room negotiating my contract with all these seasoned baseball men. I knew nothing about contracts except what one of my high school teammates had told me. He said to make sure they threw in money for a college education. With that in mind, when the Phils offered $50,000, I said they'd have to add $20,000 for college. They telephoned back to Philly and got the OK, so I signed."

Larry had only seen one major league game in his life. In 1969, his grandfather took him to Seattle for a Seattle Pilots (who later became the Milwaukee Brewers) game. LC himself knew little if anything about the East Coast clubs.

"To be honest, I didn't watch baseball," Larry confesses. "Back then, baseball didn't get the national coverage it gets now. Besides, I would always rather have gone out to hunt and fish than sit and watch a game. I loved to play the game, but I wasn't much of a spectator."

Larry believes his lack of knowledge about major league personnel helped him be assimilated.

"I didn't know who people like Steve Carlton were," LC admits. "I wasn't intimidated by him or other big stars. I would have been if I knew how great they were. Anyway, right after I signed, the Phils told me I had to fly out to Philadelphia. So there I was—on my way to Philadelphia a few days after high school graduation."

Larry had a good career in the Quaker City (83-71 with a 3.78 ERA) despite nagging back problems. LC came up from the minors for brief stints with the Phils in both '73 (34 1/3 innings) and '74 (23 innings). He stayed with the parent club for good in '75. That year, LC went 11-6 with a 3.67 ERA in 171 2/3 innings.

"I was fortunate," LC reminisces. "We had positive influences on the team like Steve Carlton and Tim McCarver. They steered a young guy like me in the right direction. That doesn't always happen. Baseball has some bad actors, too.

"They were my favorite years. We had so much fun on that club back then. It was the disco-dancing era. I took disco-dancing lessons, and ended up giving them in the clubhouse. Guys like Jim Kaat came to Philly and cut loose like they never did before. We took Kitty [Kaat] out disco dancing with us after the game. He had a great time. The whole club did."

LC followed '75 with an almost identical season: 13-8, 3.68 ERA in 168 2/3 innings. His biggest year was 1978 when he won 19 games against only six losses. The following year, despite lowering his ERA from 4.06 to 3.24, he pitched in bad luck and managed only a 13-14 record.

"I really started having back problems and arm problems in those days," LC confesses. "I had five elbow operations in all. I had 25 spurs and

"We had so much fun [in the 1970s]. It was the disco-dancing era. I took disco-dancing lessons, and ended up giving them in the clubhouse. Guys like Jim Kaat came to Philly and cut loose like they never did before."

[LARRY CHRISTENSON—FORMER PHILLIES PITCHER]

bone chips. I went to a number of different doctors, but my arm was never right again."

After tossing 228 innings in 1978, LC's injuries reduced his workload to 106, 73 2/3, and 106 innings respectively over the ensuing three seasons. He bounced back in 1982 with a full season of work. He twirled 223 innings and logged a 9-10 mark. But 1983 when the Phils won the pennant, turned out to be LC's swan song.

"At that point, I had to lift my right arm up with my left hand," Larry recalls. "I was throwing a shutout for five innings against San Diego in my last appearance. My arm was going into spasms in the dugout. Pete Rose came to the mound at one point and asked me, 'How the hell can you throw so hard with your arm like that?' Our trainer Jeff Cooper came out and wouldn't allow me to continue. That was it. Tony Gwynn got the last hit off me."

LC pitched only 48 1/3 innings in '83. He closed his career with a 2-4 mark and 3.91 ERA. He wasn't on the roster for the postseason.

Larry frequently returns to the great Northwest, his native stomping grounds, for vacations. Nonetheless, he has chosen Philadelphia as his home.

"I'm delighted I got a chance to play in Philadelphia. I sincerely believe I played with the greatest organization in the best city with the best people anywhere. I like it here."

Today, Larry Christenson is the principle in Christenson Investment Partners. He has two daughters, Libby and Claire. Libby's full name is Bentley Elizabeth—a name that Tug McGraw came up with.

Tug and LC remained close friends long after their playing careers. LC came back from a vacation in Washington on August 31, 2004, to serve as celebrity bartender when Tug's foundation for brain cancer staged a benefit at McFadden's in Citizens Bank Park.

"I'm always happy to do something for the people of Philadelphia." LC wraps up. "They've been good to me."

CLAY DALRYMPLE

Clay Dalrymple is a name that doesn't pop up too often when sport talk drifts to Phillie legends. The Dalrymple name *does* pop up however, if you happen to be watching a Mike Tollin production.

Mike Tollin is a Hollywood producer/director who lives in Beverly Hills. Tollin makes TV shows such as *ARLI$$* and movies such as *Summer Catch* and *Radio*. At least that's what he does nowadays. When he was cutting his teeth in the film industry, one of the things he did was to make videos for the Phillies. Tollin did *Whatever It Takes, Dude*, the video story of the 1993 pennant winners, narrated by Lenny Dykstra.

Mike is a Philly expatriate. He grew up in the Main Line and headed off to Stanford for college. He remains an ardent Phillies fan.

"I died in 1964," Tollin asserts. "But I never stopped believing in the Phils. They'll be my team forever. As for Clay Dalrymple—you know how it is. When you're a Philly kid, you always have a favorite Phillie. Well, Clay Dalrymple was mine."

That's why you encounter characters named "Dalrymple" in *ARLI$$* episodes. That's why the

Born: December 3, 1936, Chico, California
Position: Catcher
Years with the Phillies: 1960-1968
Uniform Number: 11
Major League Stats: .233, 55 HR, 327 RBI
• Dalrymple played in the 1969 World Series for Baltimore and batted 1.000 (two hits in two at bats)

character "Miles Dalrymple" portrayed by actor Mark Blucas appeared in Tollin's movie *Summer Catch*. Naming his characters "Dalrymple" is Mike Tollin's subtle homage to the understated, and for the most part unheralded, hero of his childhood.

Clay Dalrymple is still understated. You can ferret him out by heading up to the remote outposts of the northwest coast.

"I live in Golden Beach, Oregon," Clay Dalrymple reports. "Yeah, we're remote up here. It's great. The nearest town is about 27 miles away. Y'know why? That's the distance a stagecoach could travel back in the heyday of stagecoaches. The towns up here developed at the stagecoach stops. Bobby Doerr, the Hall of Famer, lives in the next town over. We've talked on the phone but haven't managed to get together yet.

Left: Clay Dalrymple's name keeps popping up in Hollywood more than 30 years after his final game as a Philly. The reason: producer/director and Philadelphia native Mike Tollin considers Dalrymple his favorite Philly.
Courtesy of the Philadelphia Phillies

"I'm completely retired. My wife and I lead a quiet life. We go fishing practically every day. I caught a 33-pound salmon yesterday. My freezer's full of salmon. Life is good."

Clay Dalrymple is a native Californian. He played at Chico State and was signed by Sacramento in 1956.

"They were a minor-league team," Clay explains. "They had no affiliation with a big league club. I played for the Amarillo Gold Sox in '56 and '57. Then Sacramento brought me up there in '58. They had a working agreement with Milwaukee, so the Braves invited me to spring training in '59. At the time, they had a great team and a great catcher, Del Crandall. I didn't see much opportunity for

screamed, 'Sonuvabitch! It took me 15 years to learn how to hit that pitch going *down*. I need 15 more to learn how to hit it going *up!*'

Jim Coker was the starting catcher in Dalrymple's first year in the Quaker City.

"Jim was a real scrapper," Clay remembers. "He didn't have a lot of talent, but he was scrappy. I think he was always a little cool to me cause he thought I was out for his job."

The Phils had been very stable at the catching position since 1945 when Andy Seminick took over. Seminick held the starting post till 1952 when Smoky Burgess, known as the "Little Round Man," manned it for the next three years. The Phils dealt Smoky to Cincinnati after he had hit .368. Go fig-

"I was in Philly a long time—too long. I had a good year at the plate in '62. . . . But then, for some reason, I developed a hitch in my swing. . . . I never fixed the problem the rest of my career. I just stopped hitting."

[CLAY DALRYMPLE—FORMER PHILLIES CATCHER]

myself with the Braves with Crandall there. I was happy when the Phils drafted me in 1960. I knew I had a chance to play with the Phillies.

"Philly didn't have the team Milwaukee had—not by a long shot. I found that out quick. The Phils were rebuilding when I got there. One of the first memories I have was an incident with Bobby Del Greco, one of our outfielders. Bobby was batting against a pitcher who threw submarine style. This guy's curve ball rose instead of sinking like the normal curve ball. The guy struck Bobby out. Bobby walked back to the dugout, heaved his bat, and

ure. Seminick returned to the post for a year before passing the baton to Stan Lopata. Big Stosh caught for the next three years. When Stosh left for Milwaukee in 1959, Carl Sawatski became the starter for a single year. Coker followed Sawatski and batted a measly .214. Dalrymple took over in 1961 and returned stability to the position. Clay apparently had impressed manager Gene Mauch in 1960 with his 12 pinch hits, tops on Mauch's woeful squad.

Fans didn't expect much of Dalrymple. He had only 158 plate appearances in 1960. Furthermore, the apparent instability at catcher—three different starting catchers in as many years—mirrored the team's general funk. The Phils were 64-90 in 1959 and 59-95 in 1960.

But Clay Dalrymple was in Philly to stay. Dalrymple remained the Phils starting catcher for the next seven years. In the decade of the '60s, only Johnny Callison and Tony Gonzalez boast more years as a Phillies starter.

In the Phillies' pantheon of catchers, Clay ranks fifth on the Phils' all-time list for games played. His 944 games as a catcher falls only 21 games short of the 965 games that the No. 3 place-holder Darren Daulton caught.

"I was in Philly a long time—too long," Clay chuckles. "I had a good year at the plate in '62. I hit 11 homers and batted .276. I had 10 homers the next year. But then, for some reason, I developed a hitch in my swing—just one of those mechanical things. We didn't have a hitting coach. We didn't have videos, either. I never fixed the problem the rest of my career. I just stopped hitting. The fans were brutal to me towards the end. Eventually I told the Phils, 'You should trade me. I'm not doing you any good here.' They did. I went to Baltimore and got to play on some really outstanding teams. We were in the World Series all three years I was there. We only won one Series. We beat the Big Red Machine in 1970.

"The Pirates beat us in 1971. Clemente killed us. Roberto was the greatest baseball player I ever played against—greater than Mays and Aaron. He could just tear up an opponent. I only saw one pitcher who could get him out. That was Ruben Gomez—yeah, Ruben Gomez of all people. Ruben didn't have any velocity and didn't have good stuff. He used to insist that he could handle Clemente. I thought he was crazy, but then I watched him. He actually did! He'd throw the first two pitches on the outside corner. Then his third pitch would be a foot and a half inside. Clemente swung at it every time and couldn't handle it.

"Baseball's a funny game. Johnny Callison couldn't handle Coot Veale, the Pirate's big lefty. Of course, neither could anyone else! Veale was huge. He wore glasses. He used to fan himself with his glove and peer in for the sign. He was intimidating. Mauch would sit me and the other lefthanded hitters out against Veale. Johnny stayed in the game and had to face him. One day I was encouraging Johnny before a game against Veale. I told him, 'Just stay in there against him and look for a fastball early.' Johnny said, 'Yeah, you SOB. That's easy for you to say. You don't have to *face* him.' Well as it turned out, Mauch sent me in to catch that day and I had to hit against Veale. I went up and looked for a fastball. I got one right away and hit it out. I came back and looked all over the dugout and clubhouse for Johnny that inning. I looked for him for the next few innings. I couldn't find him. He was hiding from me. When I finally caught up to him, I told him, 'See what I mean?'"

They were the kinds of episodes that made Clay Dalrymple a hero in the eyes of Hollywood's Mike Tollin. When told about his renaissance in the cinema, Clay said he wasn't aware that an ex-fan living a thousand miles down the coast was immortalizing him. Actually it's not surprising. Golden Beach doesn't have a single movie theatre. But it sure has a lot of salmon.

DARREN DAULTON

Darren (Dutch) Daulton may be the greatest self-made star ever to wear Phillies pinstripes. His record is marred by a succession of injuries that hindered his longevity and consistency.

Dutch was a high school state wrestling champion from Arkansas City, Kansas, when the Phils selected him in the 27th round of the 1980 draft.

"I had to keep my weight down in high school," Dutch reflects. "I wrestled at about 140 or 150 pounds, so I had to keep my weight around there. I played baseball and football, too, but I couldn't really gain a lot of weight because of my commitment to wrestling. When I got out of high school, I had to do the opposite. I had to beef up so I could be a major-league catcher."

Dutch was drafted by the Phils out of high school. But why would a major league team even bother to draft a 150-pound catcher?

"The Phils drafted me because they saw my parents," Daulton laughs. "My dad is about 6-7 and my mom is 5-11. They figured I'd grow."

The euphoria of being drafted hadn't subsided before the realization that Dutch had to beef up set in. He had to beef up real fast.

Born: January 3, 1962, Arkansas City, Kansas
Position: Catcher, Right Field
Years with the Phillies: 1983-1997
Uniform Number: 10
Major League Stats: .245, 137 HR, 588 RBI
Phillies Postseason Stats: '93 NLCS: .263, 1 HR, 3 RBI; '93 World Series: .217, 1 HR, 4 RBI
Honors:
- NL All-Star, 1992, 1995, starter in 1993
- NL RBI leader in 1992
- Won Silver Slugger Award in 1992
- Voted Philadelphia Sportswriters 1992 Philadelphia Professional Athlete of the Year

"The Phillies had drafted a big catcher named Lebo Powell from Pensacola, Florida in the first round that year," Daulton says. "When I reported to my first assignment in Helena, Montana, I was excited and nervous being away from home. I noticed this huge guy on the same plane as me. I couldn't help noticing him. He was huge. When we got off the plane, he yanked his bag from the overhead compartment and I saw the nametag: 'Lebo Powell.' I knew I had to hit the weight room real soon and real often."

Dutch hit the weight room. He chiseled his body to 200-plus pounds. He arrived on the Philadelphia Phillies scene in the early '80s, a pro-

Left: Darren Daulton weighed only 150 pounds when the Phillies drafted him out of high school in 1980. After adding more than 50 pounds in the weight room, "Dutch" gained enough power to become the 1992 National League RBI leader.
Courtesy of the Philadelphia Phillies

pitious time for catchers. Bob Boone was in his declining years. Boonie had been the Phils' starting catcher since 1972. He backstopped more games than any other catcher in Phillie history with the exception of Red Dooin (Whose nickname was *not* "What's"). However Boone had passed his zenith. His average dipped precipitously to .229 and .211 in 1981 and 1982. The Phils started searching—perhaps a bit desperately—for a new backstop. Dutch was in the fray for Boone's spot. Despite mediocre minor-league batting averages from 1980 through 1983 (.200, .230, .241, and .262), Dutch was called up to the Phils from Reading at the end of the 1983 season. As a side note, Dutch was brought up along with Juan Samuel and Jeff Stone. The call-ups botched Reading's run for an Eastern League crown. Reading went 96-44 that season—the finest record in the franchise's history. Years later, *Baseball America* ranked the '83 Reading squad as the 62nd best minor league team in history.

After that brief taste of the big time, Daulton was assigned to Portland. He batted a crisp .298. However, he was hampered all season by tendonitis and an irritated nerve in his right shoulder—the first of a never-ending succession of injuries that plagued him his entire year. He missed half the following season with a strained right shoulder. Again the Phils called him up at season's end. He made 103 plate appearances that season as a Philadelphia Phillie and slammed four homers. However, his average was a measly .204.

"Dutch was one determined kid," broadcaster Harry Kalas chimes. "He faced nothing but injuries when he was coming up. He wasn't putting up impressive numbers because he was always hurting. The Phils kept trying to land other catchers the whole time Dutch was in the minors. Dutch didn't get a warm feeling about his future with the Phils."

The Phils paraded a host of catchers through their ranks in the eighties. Bo Diaz and Ozzie Virgil shared the post through '85. John Russell was on board from '84-'88, and Lance Parrish brought his big name and big salary over from Detroit in '87 and '88. These guys were hardly slugs. Two of them landed spots on All-Star teams: Virgil in '85 and Parrish in '88.

Meanwhile, Daulton was struggling to keep off the disabled list. He wasn't very successful. In 1986, his season crashed to an inglorious close in late June when Mike Heath slid into his left knee on a play at the plate. Dutch tore his cruciate ligament on the play. He didn't return to action till late May, 1987. The following season, he missed the last month after he punched the wall in the video room in frustration.

"Yeah, that was a little embarrassing. They were bad days for me and the Phillies," Dutch explains. "We didn't have the right attitude in our clubhouse, and I wasn't going too well myself. It was a dumb thing to do, but it happened."

Dutch was coming into his own in 1990, mostly because he didn't land on the disabled list for the first time in six years. He upped his average to a respectable .268 and banged a career-high 12 homers and 57 RBIs. He led all NL catchers in games, walks, runs, doubles, on-base percentage, and assists. Among catchers, he was tied for the lead in homers and double plays. He also stole seven bases in eight attempts. He finally seemed on track to emerge as a solid star.

Then came the car accident. Dutch and teammate Lenny Dykstra were returning from Dutch's bachelor party when their car went out of control. They were fortunate to survive. Daulton wallowed on the disabled list from May 6 through May 21 with a broken left eye socket. He returned for one week before returning once more to the DL. He was

> **"Dutch was one determined kid. He faced nothing but injuries when he was coming up. He wasn't putting up impressive numbers because he was always hurting. The Phils kept trying to land other catchers the whole time Dutch was in the minors. Dutch didn't get a warm feeling about his future with the Phils."**
>
> [HARRY KALAS—PHILLIES BROADCASTER]

suffering from stiffness in his neck and upper back—lingering effects of the collision. He remained on the DL till June 18. When Daulton returned to active duty, he eked out a sub-Mendoza line batting average of .198 to complement a respectable total of 12 homers.

In 1992, things finally came together for Dutch. His long suffering, self-belief, patience, and hard work paid off. He became only the fourth catcher in Major League history to win an RBI title (the other three are Hall of Famers—Roy Campanella, 1953; Johnny Bench, 1970, '72, and '74; and Gary Carter, 1984). Daulton was so efficient and reliable in the clutch that he achieved what *no* other National Leaguer has ever done. He won an RBI title with fewer than 500 at-bats (his AL counterparts are familiar names: Roger Maris and Babe Ruth—the Babe did it three times). Daulton became the first Phillie catcher ever to win the Silver Slugger Award. He was selected to the All Star game and voted the Philadelphia Sportswriters' Philadelphia Professional Athlete of the Year.

The following spring, Daulton inked an $18.5 million contract—largest in Phillies' history up to that point. The signing was controversial among Quaker City sport fans. The hometowners had watched Daulton play for years, with only one starring season to show for his efforts. The Phillies' brass made the offer with more global consequences in mind.

"I'm convinced that when the Phillies gave Dutch that big salary, our '93 team came together more than ever before," Dave Hollins concedes. "Everybody looked up to Dutch as the leader. He had been with the organization since 1980. He had his ups and downs and he took his knocks. But he hung in there, because that's the kind of competitor he is. Everybody in that '93 clubhouse was aware of the kind of pain Dutch had endured for years. When he finally got a straight shot at playing a full season in '92, he came up big.

"We all interpreted that great offer by the Phils as a sign of loyalty and commitment to their players—not only to Dutch but to the whole team. There was a 'Phillie' feeling. We were a close-knit group. That move by the Phils brought us even closer. Dutch had fought a long, hard battle to earn the status he achieved in '92. The Phils were showing that they were rewarding him and backing him all the way."

"**Everybody looked up to Dutch as the leader. He had been with the organization since 1980. He had his ups and downs and he took his knocks. But he hung in there, because that's the kind of competitor he is. Everybody in that '93 clubhouse was aware of the kind of pain Dutch had endured for years. When he finally got a straight shot at playing a full season in '92, he came up big.**"

[DAVE HOLLINS—FORMER PHILLIES THIRD BASEMAN]

Dutch followed up his '92 success with another 100-plus RBI season. He was the uncontested leader of the Phils' pennant-winning '93 group of gypsies, tramps, and thieves. That campaign was destined to be his last great full season. Injuries again took him down. Dutch's promising 1994 season ended in mid-June when he broke his clavicle. He was having his finest year ever when he went down. Dutch was hitting .300 with 15 homers and 56 RBIs in only 257 at-bats.

Things got worse the following season. Daulton suffered a torn anterior cruciate ligament necessitat-

Left: Not simply an offensive catcher, Darren Daulton led National League catchers in assists and double plays in 1990. He also was a leader for the over-achieving 1993 staff that carried the Phillies to Game 6 of the World Series.
Stephen Dunn/Getty Images

ing his seventh knee surgery. In 1996, he appeared in only five games. The following year, Dutch faced a sad reality.

"Dutch was honest," Dan Stephenson, close friend and head of the Phillies video department, says. "He told the brass, 'I've been a bad major league catcher and a good major league catcher. I know the difference. And I can't be a good major league catcher anymore.' That was straight-up Dutch."

The Phils relocated him to right field and worked young Mike Lieberthal into their lineup as catcher. In August, the out-of-contention Phillies dealt Dutch to the Florida Marlins who were in the thick of a pennant race.

"I can't overemphasize the role Darren Daulton played in winning that World Series for us," Marlin manager Jim Leyland stresses. "His leadership and experience was just what our club needed to get them over the top. I honestly believe we wouldn't have won it all if we hadn't acquired Dutch."

Dutch hit .389 in that World Series for the Marlins. He called it quits after the season. He was 37 at the time. He had played all but 52 of his 1,161 major-league games as a Phillie. In the current Phils' record book, Darren Daulton places third on the Phils' all-time list of games played (965) as a catcher, right behind Bob Boone.

JIM EISENREICH

Philadelphia didn't know much about Jim Eisenreich when he arrived in Philly in 1993—except that he was *not* the guy the fans were looking for. Going back to the "Wheeze Kids"—the name given the pennant-winning '83 Phils—the Fightins managed only one winning campaign over the next decade. They finished in the top half of their division only twice.

At the dawn of the '92 campaign, the Phils were brimming with promise. Hopes had been brightened in the '91 season by an astounding 13-game win streak. The Phillies managed a third-place finish that season. However, things went sour right off the bat on opening day '92. Lenny Dykstra fractured the styloid bone on his left arm when Greg Maddux plunked him in the Dude's first at-bat of the season. The Phils' season tanked from there on. They limped in dead last at season's end. The local wish doctors, exasperated by the disappointing season, prescribed a glitzy marquis star to cure the team's ill. Jim Eisenreich, a quiet, singles-doubles-hitter was not the requested medicine. Nor was anyone else the Phils brought in that off season.

Pete Incaviglia, Milt Thompson, Danny Jackson, and Larry Andersen all became Phillies

Left: Jim Eisenreich batted .318 for the Phillies in 1993, the first of his four consecutive .300-plus seasons in a Phillies uniform.
Stephen Dunn/Getty Images

Born: April 18, 1959, St. Cloud, Minnesota
Position: Outfield
Years with the Phillies: 1993-1996
Uniform Number: 8
Major League Stats: .290, 52 HR, 477 RBI
Phillies Playoff Stats: 1993 NLCS: .133, 0 HR, 1 RBI. 1993 World Series: .231, 1 HR, 7 RBI
Honors:
• First winner of Tony Conigliaro Award (1991) presented to a ML player who has overcome adversity through spirit, determination, and courage
• 1993 Most Courageous Athlete, Philadelphia Sportswriters Association

prior to the '93 season. None of them were considered baseball's elite, but as a group, they plugged the multiple holes that shipwrecked the '92 squad.

Eisy quickly became a fan favorite in '93. Jim's character and fortitude won the Philly fans over. Eisy had overcome Tourette Syndrome, a little understood disease that causes involuntary tics, twitches, and outbursts.

"I had Tourette Syndrome all my life. I never knew what it was. I was never diagnosed till I was 23," Jim Eisenreich explains. "By the time I was 25, the disease was so bad I thought I was done with baseball."

Minnesota drafted Eisy in the 16th round in 1980. He wound up being the Appalachian League's co-player of the year that same year. In his second minor-league season, he led the Midwest League in doubles and games played. He was second in average, RBIs, runs, and total bases. His performance landed him on a Major League roster slot on

> ## "I spent the happiest season of my life in Philly in 1993. Those guys were sincere. They were rough and ready but they had good hearts. They accepted me straight up. No one danced around the Tourette Syndrome and I felt so much more welcome because of the way they handled it."
>
> [JIM EISENREICH—FORMER PHILLIES OUTFIELDER]

Opening Day 1982—an amazingly fast ascent for an unheralded player. Eisy had also been stellar in spring training that year.

Jim's major-league career got off to a fine start. He hit in eight of his first nine games. Then tragedy struck.

"I told Billy Gardner, my manager, I couldn't continue," Jim recalls. On June 11, 1982, Eisenreich placed himself on the disabled list for the first time because of Tourette Syndrome. He was batting .303 at the time.

In '83, the nightmare repeated. Again Eisenreich was on the opening-day Twins' roster.

On the second day of the season, however, he was again compelled to step down. The Tourette Syndrome had resurfaced. The following season, Eisy got 12 games in before withdrawing. This time, he placed himself on the voluntary retired list.

Jim Eisenreich is nothing if not a battler. He remained out of baseball for three seasons, only to resurface with Kansas City in 1987. In 1988, he bounced between Kansas City and their Omaha minor league affiliate. Then in 1989, he launched a breakout campaign, leading the Royals in average, doubles, stolen bases, and triples.

As a Royal, Eisy batted .293, .280, and .301 successively from 1989 through 1991. When his average slipped to .269 in 1992, the Royals dealt him to the Phils.

"I had no idea what it was going to be like in that crazy Phillies clubhouse," Eisy chuckles. "Those guys had quite a reputation with John Kruk, Lenny Dykstra, Mitch Williams, Dutch Daulton. I didn't know how they'd accept me. I couldn't have been more pleased, though. I spent the happiest season of my life in Philly in 1993. Those guys were sincere. They were rough and ready but they had good hearts. They accepted me straight up. No one danced around the Tourette Syndrome and I felt so much more welcome because of the way they handled it."

Straight up is one way to put it. In what would "normally" (if anything about the '93 Phils could be considered normal) be a human resource department's nightmare, John Kruk tagged Eisy

"Dahmer," because of the grimaces and tics the disease caused. As Eisy put it, though, they were no more brutal on him than anyone else. Eisy gave it right back. Everyone stayed loose and they all had fun in the process. The bottom line was that Eisy was accepted as a member of the group for the first time. He wasn't treated as someone different.

"In the middle of the season, my wife, Leann, went up to Kruk and said, 'John Kruk, I hate you,'" Eisy explains. "Kruk had this look like he had been caught red-handed doing something wrong. Then Leann let him off the hook saying, 'We used to get to sleep at a normal hour. Now we're up till one in the morning because Jim has to tell me all the crazy things that happened that day!' You know what Krukker answered? 'That's cause Jim has less problems than the rest of us. He's the only normal one around here.'"

Eisy hit .318 in '93. He platooned in right field with Wes Chamberlain, and delivered numerous clutch hits and clutch plays. He is probably best remembered for his clutch three-run third-inning homer in Game 2 of the World Series.

Eisy's .318 season in '93 proved to be no fluke. It was the first of four consecutive .300 seasons as a Phil. In his final season in Phillie pinstripes, Eisy hit a torrid .361. Throughout his impressive stint as a Phil, he remained a fan favorite because of his unwavering effort on the field, and his courage in overcoming his affliction.

In 1997, Eisy was dealt to the Florida Marlins. Along with '93-Phillie mate Darren Daulton, Jim Eisenreich helped the Marlins win the World Series ring that had eluded the Phils in 1993.

Eisy played only one more year after '97, splitting time between the Marlins and Dodgers. He retired with an impressive .290 career average. Since his retirement, Jim and wife Leann have been devoting their time and energy to helping those afflicted with Tourette Syndrome and raising funds for its cure and treatment.

Below: Jim Eisenreich inspired others by overcoming Tourette Syndrome to become a successful major-league ballplayer. *Courtesy of the Philadelphia Phillies*

DEL ENNIS

Here's a trivia question that might throw a lot of Philly fans. Everybody knows that Mike Schmidt ranks first on the Phils' all-time home run list. *Duh.* But who ranks second? No, it's not Chuck Klein and it's not Greg Luzinski. They rank three and four, respectively. The No. 2 spot belongs to Delmer Ennis. That's not news to the dyed-in-the-wool Phillie fan. But this one is. Who is the only Phil who ranks in the club's all-time top ten in singles, doubles, triples, and home runs? Answer: Del Ennis.

Given his accomplishments as a Philadelphia Phillie, it's not hard to understand why number 14, the jersey Ennis wore, is retired. Number 14 is retired in the name of Jim Bunning, not Del Ennis. Bunning deserves the honor. But so does Ennis.

Ennis is the Phillie that Philly fans tend to forget. Given that Ennis is a native son and graduate of Olney High School, the effacement of Del Ennis is downright enigmatic.

LIZ ENNIS, DEL'S WIDOW: "Del could never understand the reaction of the Phillies' fans. He tried to say it didn't bother him, but it did."

Left: Despite putting up offensive numbers matched only by Mike Schmidt in Phillies history, Del Ennis was never a fan favorite.
Brace Photo

Born: June 8, 1925, Philadelphia, Penn.
Died: February 8, 1996, Huntingdon Valley, Penn.
Position: Outfield
Years with the Phillies: 1946-1956
Uniform Number: 14
Major League Stats: .284, 288 HR, 1,284 RBI
Phillies Playoff Stats: 1950 World Series: .143, 0 HR, 0 RBI
Honors:
• NL Phillie All-Star, 1946, 1951 (starter), 1955 (starter)
• 1946 *Sporting News* Rookie of the Year
• Inducted into the Philadelphia Wall of Fame in 1982
• Chosen as an outfielder for Phillies All-Centennial Team in 1983

The "it" that Liz Ennis is referring to is the *booing.* Ennis was the target of what was, arguably, the greatest onslaught of boos Philly fans ever rained down on a home-team player.

LIZ ENNIS: "Del always thought he could have played better if the hometown fans had treated him with more respect and love. It's tough to go out every day, give your all, and then get booed for every move you make. It *has* to affect your performance."

And Ennis's performance as a Phil was nothing short of sterling. He played 11 years for the Fightins. In his prime, he was one of the league's biggest stars. Over the nine-year period from 1949-1957, only one player in all of baseball, Stan Musial, knocked in more runs than Del. Musial topped Del's total by nine—in other words, about one

"Del always thought he could have played better if the home-town fans had treated him with more respect and love."

[LIZ ENNIS—DEL ENNIS'S WIDOW]

more RBI per year. Trailing Del on that RBI list are a string of Hall of Famers like Duke Snider, Jackie Robinson, Yogi Berra, Roy Campanella, and Ralph Kiner as well as ballyhooed stars like Carl Furillo, Ted Kluszewski, Gil Hodges, and the author of "Baseball's Greatest Moment," Bobby Thomson.

Over that same '49-'57 period, Ennis ranked eighth in most home runs hit in the NL. The only Phillie player in history who fares better over a nine-year reign is Mike Schmidt. If we compare Michael Jack's most productive nine-year consecutive span, 1979-1987, we find that Schmidt led the major-league pack in both home runs and RBIs. But Schmidt ranked number 15 in batting average, while Ennis placed 11th.

That comparison doesn't diminish what Schmidt accomplished, nor does it suggest that Ennis was as potent at the plate as Schmidt. The comparison does underscore that Ennis was a player who could and did carry a team. Twice in 1950 he homered in four consecutive games. He's the only Phil besides Schmidt to accomplish that feat more than once in the same season. When the Phils won

the 1950 pennant, Del led the NL in RBIs with 126 (Hall of Famer Ralph Kiner was a distant second with 118). Ennis's 31 homers were fifth best in the NL. His .311 average ranked fourth in the NL. Yet despite placing in the NL's top five in those three key offensive categories, Ennis was overlooked for the 1950 All-Star squad. Four of his teammates were selected: Ashburn, Roberts, Sisler, and Konstanty. However, Ennis, who led the Whiz Kids in every offensive category but triples, walks, and stolen bases (Ashburn led in those three), was shunned.

Ennis was the Mike Schmidt of the '50s Phillies. Actually, Del led the Phils in RBIs more seasons than Schmidt did. Ennis led ten times, Schmidt nine.

Del Ennis held his own—and then some—against the top players of his day. Still he was booed unmercifully in his own hometown. The reasons were never clear.

LIZ ENNIS: "We owned a bowling alley for years after Del retired. People were forever coming up to Del and saying things like, 'I used to boo you like crazy back in Connie Mack Stadium.' They'd say it like it was funny or amusing. People have no idea how it hurt Del to hear that. He tried to pass it off like it was just part of the game. But it bothered him. He loved Philadelphia. He never wanted to live anywhere else. We vacationed in Florida a lot. Eventually we owned some greyhound racing dogs down there. I know there's a lot of concern about cruelty to those animals. We made sure that didn't happen to ours. We didn't get involved in the business until we were absolutely certain our animals would be treated properly and humanely by a reputable trainer. And I made sure when we got out of the business that every one of our dogs was given a good home.

"Anyway, even though we had business ties in Florida, Del never wanted to leave Philly. He was part of the Phils' very first Phantasy Camp in Clearwater. Phantay camp is for regular fans who want to experience first hand what it's like to play major league baseball. Retired ballplayers like Del go down and coach and manage the campers. Everybody has a great time. Del had a ball. But he never wanted to stay in Florida permanently. He was a Philly person, despite the booing he got here.

"When the Phils traded him to St. Louis, Del was deeply hurt. He couldn't believe it. They traded him for Rip Repulski and Bobby Joe Morgan. It had to be the worst trade the Phils ever made! Did you know Del got more RBIs than Stan Musial the year after he was traded? Stan was his good friend in St. Louis. The two of them roomed together. But Del never once considered moving to St. Louis. He kept an apartment there during the season. That was it. After the season, he came back to Philly."

Del Ennis left an impressive legacy with the Phils. He was one of only seven Phils ever selected to the All-Star team as a rookie. Ennis was the first Phillie ever to start an All Star game in left field. He was also the first Phillie ever to win a Rookie of the Year Award (Ennis and Ashburn each won the TSN Rookie of the Year Award).

In 1982, Del became the fifth Phil inducted into the Philadelphia Wall of Fame. The tradition, which was inaugurated at Veterans Stadium in 1978, has carried over to Citizens Bank Park. Each year a Phillie great is inducted. At the Vet, a Phillie and a Philadelphia Athletic were inducted each year. Unfortunately, now that the original Wall of Fame from the Vet has physically been moved over to Citizens Bank Park, the Phils no longer enshrine an Athletic (the Philadelphia A's Wall of Fame is now housed in the Philadelphia Athletics Museum in Hatboro, Pennsylvania). Incidentally, #14 Jim Bunning was the Phil selected for the Wall of Fame the year after Del Ennis.

Del Ennis was also selected as the all-century Philadelphia Phillie left fielder. He topped Greg Luzinski and Sherry Magee, both of whom are Phillie legends.

Ennis detractors tag him as a huge liability in the field. His record contradicts the charge. Five times he recorded 14 assists, a feat no other Phillie outfielder since 1927 can claim (1927 marked the fifth season that Cy Williams recorded 14 or more outfield assists).

Ennis's record speaks for itself. His accomplishments make the booing enigmatic—as enigmatic as why Phillie uniform #14 isn't retired in both Del Ennis's and Jim Bunning's name.

Phillies Rookie All-Stars

Del Ennis	OF	1946	Juan Samuel	2B	1984
Richie Ashburn	OF	1948	Tyler Green	P	1995
Jack Sanford	P	1957	Jimmy Rollins	SS	2001
Ray Culp	P	1963			

BILL GILES

"**I**'ve always viewed baseball as entertainment."

They're the words Bill Giles lives by. He brings a sense of humor and a rare sentimentality to his profession. Given his enviable background—enviable to every baseball-loving kid in the country—Giles also brings an abiding understanding and love of the sport to an industry that is often dismissed as cold and uncaring. What is his enviable background? Bill Giles is the son of a former National League president. The position of NL president dates back to 1876, when Morgan G. Bulkeley became the first to hold the position. Bill's dad, Warren Giles, held the post for 18 years, a longer tenure than any of his 16 predecessors.

From 1946-1951, prior to becoming National League president, Warren Giles was president and general manager of the Cincinnati Reds. Consequently, young Bill Giles had the kind of access that kids all over the country would have willingly surrendered their only Topps' Mickey Mantle card for.

Bill's mom died when he was only nine. The young Giles spent most of his days tagging after his

dad at the old Crosley Field in Cincinnati. Bill's constancy at the park paid off. His first "job" wound up being a baseball job. At age 14, Bill was a "gopher" for the Reds public relations department.

Bill attended Denison College. After graduation, he spent three years in the Air Force as a navigator for the Strategic Air Command. Following that, he landed his first full-time job in baseball. In 1959, he served as the general manager of the Nashville Vols, a Cincinnati Reds farm club. Not many years later, he joined the Houston Colt 45s—who eventually changed their names to the Astros. With the Astros, Bill Giles held several positions: traveling secretary, publicity director, director of publicity and promotions, and vice president.

The Carpenter family, who owned the Phillies at the time, wooed him to the City of Brotherly Love in 1969. Veterans Stadium was set to debut. The Phillie franchise had suffered through a few gloomy years of second-division baseball in the late '60s. As the '70s broke, the club was anxious to break with the past in its brand new showcase stadium.

Veterans Stadium would be a grand circular multipurpose arena and the largest ballpark in the National League. The Phils brass looked to add some glitz—a foreign element in Philadelphia baseball up till then. They figured Bill Giles was the guy to do it.

And do it he did. Bill Giles introduced a new tradition of Opening Day spectacles. He brought heretofore unseen circus acts and assorted mayhem on to the diamond. He moved up the Phillies ranks quickly. Following the 1969 season, he became the VP of business operations. Within three years, he was promoted to executive VP.

When the Carpenters put the Phillies up for sale, Bill Giles had a chance to realize his personal dream to own a Major League team. Giles organized a group that purchased the team on October 29, 1981. Bill served as president of the ownership group until June 20, 1997, when he moved up to chairman.

Bill Giles developed a love of baseball early on. He coupled that love with a keen, pragmatic understanding of the American public's fickle tastes in entertainment. Giles realized that contemporary kids need more stimulation than those of the past. As business gurus preach nowadays, a satisfied customer is risky. A satisfied customer is a customer you're on the brink of losing. Businesses need to *wow*, not satisfy their customers. In the '70s, baseball started riding that wave. Bill Giles was out ahead of many in the baseball pack in embracing the need to entertain or lose customers.

BILL GILES: "Thinking of baseball as entertainment was natural for me. I saw that clearly when I got to Philly in 1970. I grew up in Cincinnati where Opening Day was treated as something sacred. For years, Cincinnati was the traditional place where the first game of the season was played. In Philly, Opening Day was treated more like just another ballgame. I believe openers should be special, a celebration that spring has arrived and baseball is back and life is good. That was the first thing I set out to do in Philly—generate some opening-day fervor."

Giles succeeded. Over the years in Philly, he has always found a way to *mach shau* in the opener. Under Giles's helm, baseballs have been dropped from hovering helicopters. Kiteman has sailed onto the field or crashed into the stands (upholding the Quaker City tradition of unsafe kite practices initiated by Ben Franklin). Cannonman has been shot out of a cannon clutching the first ball in his hand. Parachutists—including even the Phillie Phanatic—have floated into the stadium. Karl Wallenda has walked a tight rope strung across the aeries of Veterans Stadiums, and the Phillie Phanatic has slid down a 200-foot long wire to deliver the first ball.

Speaking of the Phanatic, Bill Giles dreamt up that idea, too. In the 26 years since the Phillie Phanatic first waddled into the Vet, he has become professional sports' most famous and enduring mascot.

BILL GILES: "It was back in the mid-'70s. One of our guys saw the Chicken Man down in San Diego. He came back to Philly all pumped up saying, 'We've got to do something like that here at the Vet.' I believed he was right. Getting a mascot became a personal crusade for me. I thought a mascot would open the door to lots of fun."

Giles endured the slings and arrows of outrageous—well, disbelief. Remember, this was a different era. Travel back for a moment to the '70s, when bell bottoms and clashing stripes and polka dots were *haute couture*. There *were* no mascots in baseball or any other professional sport. Giles's suggestion was bold. But time has substantiated its sagacity. We'll hear from another Phillie legend (just ask him) Dave Raymond, the original Phillie Phanatic, later in the book. For the moment, suffice it to say that the Phanatic now merits a permanent display in the Hall of Fame. No other mascot has been so honored, except for Chicken Man. Chicken Man, however, is an independent. He's not officially attached to the San Diego Padres' organization. The Phillie Phanatic—all 300 pounds of him—is a full-time Phillies employee.

Giles incorporated plenty of previously unseen entertainment into the ballgame spectacle. He has trotted pig shows, sea lions, African baboons, and dancing poodles out onto the Vet playing field. He's held mattress-stacking competitions, cash scrambles, three-legged races, postgame concerts, a toga party, and a legendary ostrich race that featured Richie Ashburn and other celebs racing ostriches around the Vet. The birds ran around as out of control as Rush Limbaugh in a Mexican pharmacy. The more things went wacko, the more the fans roared.

CHRISSY LONG, PHILS MARKETING GROUP: "We had elephants as the pregame show once. Only once. The elephants left their mark on the field, if you know what I mean. It stunk to high heaven. Our groundskeepers got much more than they bargained for. They couldn't get the stench out. The poor guys spent days trying to deodorize the grounds."

The public knows Bill Giles as the promoter. The Bill Giles the public doesn't know well is the sympathetic and approachable boss. He's unusually loyal to his employees for the baseball business. Giles has developed paternalistic or avuncular relationships with many of the Phillies personnel, including the ballplayers.

MAJE McDONNELL: "Bill is sentimental about the game of baseball. I know that personally. I had left the Phils. I was coaching at Chestnut Hill Academy in the '60s. Bill was there one day to watch a game. He recognized me from the 'old' days when he followed his father around in Cincinnati. He came up to me and said, 'Maje, you belong with the Phillies. You've been with them all your life. I want you back where you belong.' That's the way Mr. Giles feels about the franchise and the game. He's really sentimental."

People like Dutch Daulton, the Phils' All-Star catcher from the '90s, speak highly of Bill Giles, too.

DUTCH DAULTON: "I trusted Bill more than anyone in baseball. He had a relationship with the players that was different than other owners. Put it this way, to this day I call him Uncle Bill. That's how he's always treated me, like someone who cares about me personally."

Bill Giles demonstrates that he cares about Philadelphia, too. He has become an engaged citizen of his adopted city. Bill is chairman emeritus of the board of the Philadelphia Convention and Tourism Bureau and a member of the Executive Committee of the Philadelphia Chamber of Commerce. He served as president of the Boy Scouts of America and has also belonged to the board of the Pennsylvania Chamber of Commerce, the Greater Philadelphia First, and the Police Athletic League.

Bill Giles was instrumental in conceiving and bringing to fruition the Phillies dream of a new ballpark. Citizens Bank Park was one of his prized babies. With the new park and Thome-led team, Giles hopes to have pointed his franchise in the right direction for the new millennium.

TONY
GONZALEZ

The 1960 Phillies were undergoing a rebuilding program yet again. The "Fabulous Four Freshmen" of 1957—Rookie of the Year pitcher Jack Sanford, fan-favorite shortstop "Go-Go Chico" Fernandez who ignited the hometowners with his baserunning pizzazz (Chico's 18 steals ranked fifth in the NL), first sacker Ed Bouchee, who smacked 17 rookie homers and batted .293, and Harry "the Horse" Anderson who also pounded 17 rookie round-trippers in 400 at-bats—were all gone by the end of 1960.

Sanford was traded to the Giants. Personal problems forced Bouchee out of baseball. He ended his career as a .161 hitter on the lowly '62 Mets. Chico proved to be a good field/good run/no hit shortstop whose weak bat was too impotent for the Phils batting order to carry. And once Harry Anderson's hitting weaknesses were discovered and exploited, he was reduced to an easy out.

The '57 hopefuls had finished dead even at 77-77. As the members of the Fabulous Four Freshmen—who were once envisioned as the Phils' future nucleus—left town, the Phils had to initiate another rebuilding program.

An early move saw the Phils deal Harry Anderson, Wally Post, and Fred Hopke to the

Left: Tony Gonzalez was a mainstay in the Phillies' outfield during the 1960s. He led the Phils in batting average four times. *Courtesy of the Philadelphia Phillies*

> **Born:** August 28, 1936, Central Cunagua, Cuba
> **Position:** Outfield
> **Years with the Phillies:** 1960-1968
> **Uniform Number:** 25
> **Major League Stats:** .286, 103 HR, 615 RBI

Redlegs (Cincinnati called themselves the Redlegs rather than the Reds in the '60s. "Red" was a hot-button word during the Cold War). In return, they got little-known Cuban prospect Tony Gonzalez and bespectacled outfielder Lee Walls.

Cincinnati had signed Tony Gonzalez in 1957. He made his major-league debut on April 12, 1960, hitting a homer off Phillies starter Robin Roberts. Gonzalez impressed the Phils so much with that swing, they set their sights on landing him. It proved to be a good move.

In 78 games his first season as a Phillie, Gonzalez hit .299, tops on the club. He was a regular the following season, hitting .274, stroking 12 homers, and stealing 15 bases. The '61 squad finished in last place with a horrid 47-107 record. During the season, they suffered the ignominy of a 23-game losing streak. Despite their woes, the Phils had quietly assembled a hefty chunk of the nucleus of the 1964 team. Tony Gonzalez, Johnny Callison, Tony Taylor, Chris Short, Art Mahaffey,

Wes Covington, and Clay Dalrymple were all members of that '61 squad that was tested by fire.

The Mets arrived on the scene in '62. The Phils vaulted over their backs to escape the basement for the first time since 1958. A few bright spots were starting to twinkle. Gonzalez upped

> ## "He had surprising power. Tony was the strongest guy from his forearms to his fingertips I ever met. He could rip balls the opposite way. He was just like Clemente. They both hit line drives. It seemed like Tony hit a rope every at-bat. He had tremendous power to the opposite field. The guy was really underrated."
>
> [CLAY DALRYMPLE—FORMER PHILLIES CATCHER]

his average to .302, second best on the Phils behind Don Demeter's .307. Through 1968, Gonzalez, despite being a contemporary of Dick Allen, led the Phils in batting average four different times. From 1960 through his final season as a Phil in '68, Tony batted .295.

Tony slammed 20 homers in 1962—the first and only time he ever reached that milestone.

"He had surprising power," teammate Clay Dalrymple recalls. "Tony was the strongest guy from his forearms to his fingertips I ever met. He could rip balls the opposite way. He was just like Clemente. They both hit line drives. It seemed like

Tony hit a rope every at-bat. He had tremendous power to the opposite field. The guy was really underrated."

In '62, Gonzalez also swiped 17 bases and scored 78 runs. Both were career highs. His most lasting achievement that season however happened on defense. Tony set the all-time standard (others have tied) for perfection in center field. In 114 games, he handled 268 chances without an error for a flawless 1.000 fielding percentage.

Tony followed '62 with another .300 season. His home run output dwindled to four, but his .306 average included a team-best 36 doubles (third best in the NL), 11 more than he had in any other season in his career. The year 1962 also marked the first time he played a full season— 155 games. Surprisingly, Gonzalez played only one other full season. Every other season he was platooned—a Gene Mauch measure that puzzled many fans.

"Tony had good bat speed and bat control," teammate Johnny Callison recalls. "He was an important part of our attack. I don't know why Mauch platooned him. One year Tony almost won a batting title and wound up getting platooned the next year."

"I don't think [manager] Gene Mauch liked Tony too much," Clay Dalrymple chuckles. "Gene had his ways. Tony wasn't a big guy, but he ran like he was 6'5". He took real long strides and it didn't look like he was moving fast, but he was. I don't think that sat well with Mauch. Tony took it well, though. He was always smiling and happy. One day he missed a cutoff man. When he got back to the dugout, Mauch was all over him. Tony didn't speak English very well. Finally he threw his glove and said, 'I go. I leave.' Mauch said, 'Then we won't pay you.' Tony retrieved his glove and said, 'Maybe I play a little longer!'"

In 1967, Gonzalez had a monster season, at least for batting average. He hit an Ashburn-esque .339 and lost the NL Batting Crown to Roberto Clemente. Gonzalez played against righties and lefties alike that season, appearing in 149 games. The following season he was again platooned with guys like Don Locke, a .210 hitter. Tony's average tumbled to .264, which happened to be best on the squad. The Phillies were fading fast at that point.

Notwithstanding his team-best average, the Phils were cleaning house again in 1969. The centerfielder of the future appeared to be Larry Hisle. Tony Gonzalez was surrendered to the expansion draft—the pool of players who would form the neophyte Montreal Expos and San Diego Padres. The 32-year-old Gonzalez was selected by the San Diego Padres on October 14, 1968. He was the 38th player selected in the draft.

Tony was traded during the season to the Braves who coughed up the forgettable trio of Walt Hriniak, Van Kelly, and Andy Finlay to land him. In 320 at-bats, Gonzalez batted .294 and slugged ten homers to help the Braves land an NL West Division title. In the NLCS that year, Atlanta went up against the Miracle Mets. Gonzalez started in the outfield with Hank Aaron and Rico Carty. Tony registered more plate appearances (14) than any other Brave. He slugged a homer, scored a team-best four runs and drove in two. His .357 series average tied Hank Aaron's as the club's second highest. However the Mets emerged victorious.

Tony spent most of 1970 as a Brave. Then on August 31, 1970, the California Angels purchased him. He batted .304 in 92 at-bats for the Angels during a stretch drive that fell short of a division title. Tony Gonzalez finished his career as an Angel in 1971, hitting an uncharacteristic .245 in 314 at-bats. He retired with a lifetime batting average of .286.

Tony is living in Florida today. Up until a few years ago, he participated in the Phillies' Phantasy Camp. He's still in good health and excellent shape. As Art Mahaffey observes, "I saw Tony not too long ago. He looks like he could still hit a line drive."

Above: Tony Gonzalez batted .339 in 1967, finishing second to Roberto Clemente for the National League batting crown. The next season, Gene Mauch platooned him with Don Locke.
Brace Photo

AL HOLLAND

Al Holland had Philly attitude and Philly loved him back. He was grit, spit, and fire on the diamond. Al was far from a pretty boy.

"Al used to talk about his summer teeth. 'Some 'r here, some 'r there,'" former Phil Larry Christenson says, referring to Al's Stonehenge-like dental array. "It made him look a little mean on the mound. Al was intense. He went out to do a job and he usually got the job done."

Al Holland came to the City of Brotherly Love along with Joe Morgan by way of San Francisco. Both were instrumental in the success of the Phillies' 1983 pennant-winning Wheeze Kids. Morgan was headed to the Hall of Fame. Holland was a relative unknown. However, it didn't take Holland long to click with the tough Phillie crowds.

"I loved Philly," Holland reflects. "It's a beautiful looking city with the Art Museum and all. But it's such a great blue-collar town, too. I was happy there. Philly fans take to ballplayers who bring everything to the park every day. They know the guys who do. And they're rough on the guys who don't. You can't fool Philly fans."

Al moved to Voorhees, New Jersey during the playoffs in '83. He didn't leave till '91, long after he left the Phils. He headed south back to his native Roanoke.

"I grew up down there," Al reflects. "I went to North Carolina A&T and got a degree in Recreation Administration. I was a running back there. I played baseball, too. I was drafted twice—once after my freshman year and once after my junior year. I stayed in college instead of signing. The money wasn't big enough to make me leave. The Pirates—Branch Rickey III—signed me when I graduated. I reported to Bradenton. Then I went to

Left: Al Holland, known as "Mr. T" during his days with the Phillies, was the Rolaids Relief Man of the Year in 1983.
Courtesty of the Philadelphia Phillies

Niagara Falls, and wound up playing for Salem, Virginia, four miles from my home."

Al came up to the big leagues with the Pirates in 1977. He was immediately assigned to the bullpen.

"I only played with the Pirates in '78. They traded me to the Giants in '79," he recalls. "I relieved for the Giants, too, at least from '79 through '81 I did. Then in '82 they tried to convert me to a starter. I started about nine games before I pulled a hamstring. When I healed, I asked to go back to the pen. I liked it better out there."

> ## "I basically just threw fastballs. I had a curve, but I figured I never wanted to let anyone beat me on my second-best pitch. I threw a two-seam fastball and a four-seam fastball pretty much exclusively. I figured I'd challenge each guy cause I didn't think anybody could beat me."
>
> [AL HOLLAND—FORMER PHILLIES CLOSER]

After going 7-3 with a 3.33 ERA, Al was dealt to the Phils.

"I wasn't surprised at the trade. The Giants had Greg Minton and me. I knew there was only gonna be one closer. I was happy for the opportunity in Philly. But otherwise I wouldn't have wanted to leave San Francisco. I loved that city. The fans were good. I was happy while I was there. "

Al had a monster year in his first season as a Phil. He was 8-4 and earned the *Sporting News* NL

Fireman of the Year Award as well as the Rolaids Relief Man of the Year Award. He followed his great season by pitching scoreless baseball in both the NLCS and the World Series. After recording an exciting victory over the Dodgers in the NLCS, the Phils fell short in the World Series.

"I think we kind of had an emotional letdown after we beat the Dodgers," Holland confesses. "The Dodgers beat the Phils out of a pennant in the '70s. I know that loss really stung. So beating the Dodgers in '83 was redemption not only for guys like Schmidty who had played in that series but for the city as well. I think that as a team we didn't come down from the high of winning the NLCS the way we should have. And let's face it. We came up against a good Baltimore team. Their pitching shut us down."

The following season, Al was selected to the NL All-Star team. However, the Phils slipped to fourth place (out of six) and kicked off a downward spiral that didn't stop spinning till 1993.

"I think the '83 Phils were basically put together as a one-year club," Al explains. "Right after '83, [reliever] Willie Hernandez went to Detroit. Ron Reed, another reliever, retired. In '84, we didn't have the setup men we had the year before. That meant I had to pitch longer. And we lost Joe Morgan and Pete Rose. It just wasn't the same."

Al Holland is best remembered as "Mr. T" during his days with the Phils.

Al Holland closed games for a 1983 Phillies team that advanced to the World Series before falling to Baltimore.
Focus on Sport/Getty Images

"Ed Farmer hung the Mr. T name on me," Al explains. "I was walking up the runway one night after we won a game, and Ed shouts, 'Here comes Mr. T!' Some reporters heard him and they ran with it. He was referring to the chains I wore. I really didn't wear that much gold around my neck! I had two necklaces. My wife gave me both of them."

The press ran with the Mr. T tag because the name seemed appropriate. Holland had a no-nonsense, snarling, take-no-prisoners mien on the mound.

"I basically just threw fastballs," Al continues. "I had a curve, but I figured I never wanted to let anyone beat me on my second-best pitch. I threw a two-seam fastball and a four-seam fastball pretty much exclusively. I figured I'd challenge each guy cause I didn't think anybody could beat me."

Al never again recaptured the magic of the 1983 season. He slipped to 5-10 in 1984. He split 1985 between the Phils, Pirates, and Angels. The Angels secured his services for help down the stretch, but the Halos fell a game short of the Royals. Holland's record as an Angel was 0-1, with a sparkling 1.48 ERA. The following year, he switched Yankee pinstripes.

"I spent two years with the Yanks," Al reminisces. "I ended my career with them. It happened suddenly. I threw one pitch and my career was over—just like that. My elbow blew up and never came back. I always had a goal to pitch till I was 40, but I fell short."

Al left baseball at age 35. After retirement, he substituted for awhile as a teacher at Easton High School. He continues to use his degree for a livelihood.

"When baseball season is over, I work with the Roanoke School district," Al reports. "During the season, I'm a pitching coach for the St. Louis Cardinals' minor league system. My ultimate goal is to become a big-league pitching coach. I'd like to take that challenge on next."

DAVE HOLLINS

Many Phillie fans would be surprised that the Phils did *not* nickname Dave Hollins "Headley" as an expression of his behavior. Sometimes Dave's intensity went over the top. Dave's teammate and the 2004 Phils' backup backstop Todd Pratt also marches to a different drummer. Pratt explains, "The '93 Phils called Dave 'Headley' because he has such a big head. That's basically the reason. They called me Head too. Maybe you noticed. I have a big head, too."

Hollins does have a large noggin, but his intensity is far more fabled. Edginess and unpredictability summed up his diamond persona.

"There was a 20-minute period before and after the game when you couldn't get anywhere near Head," John Kruk recalls. "He would just sit and stare into his locker and pump himself up for the game. Everyone knew to keep away."

"David was the best baserunner from first to third that I ever saw," Jim Fregosi, Phils' manager in 1993 says. "We had some great baserunners on that 1993 team. Dutch Daulton could break up a double play as well as anyone who ever played the game. But David played baseball like a linebacker. He didn't

Born: May 26, 1966, Buffalo, New York
Position: Third Base
Years with the Phillies: 1990-1995; 2002
Major League Stats: .261, 112, 482 RBI
Phillies Postseason Stats: 1993 ALCS, .200, 2 HR, 4 RBI; 1993 World Series, .261, 0 HR, 2 RBI
Honors:
• 1986 USA baseball team
• 1993 NL All-Star

have great speed but he knew how to run the bases. In his mind, the basepaths belonged to him and he would knock out anyone who got in his path."

To a man, Hollins's teammates on the pennant-winning 1993 Phillies praise his focus, concentration, and resolve. "I knew I didn't have great talent," Hollins said. "I had to work harder and try harder than the rest of the guys. I was used to hard work. That's the only way I knew. Since I didn't have the greatest talent, I felt that some opponents didn't give me respect. I felt I had something to prove every time I stepped on to the field. Certain teams, particularly the Braves, acted like I wasn't worthy to be on the same field with them. In fact, back in '93, I think they felt that way about our whole team. That attitude made me want to beat them bad every time we came up against them."

Left: Dave Hollins hit 18 home runs and drove in 93 for the 1993 Phillies.
Jonathan Daniel/Getty Images

Dave Hollins was admittedly a little rough around the edges in his early years. His play at third could be erratic. His arm was unpredictable. He had not been a highly sought amateur. He graduated from Orchard Park High School in Buffalo, New York in 1984 and played college ball for the University of South Carolina in the 1985 College World Series. He also played for the USA in the 1986 World Championships before the San Diego Padres selected him in the sixth round of the June, 1987 draft. He was assigned immediately to Spokane in the Northwest League where he finished seventh in batting with a .309 average. In his sophomore year in the minors, he became a California League All-Star with Riverside. The following year, after batting .275 for Wichita in the Texas League and leading the Mexican League in

and performed so well that he was brought up to the Phils in July. He won the Phillies "Player of the Month" honors that month by hitting five homers, driving in 13, and achieving an .816 slugging average. He took over the starting third baseman job from incumbent Charlie Hayes, who was traded the following year.

Headly continued an ongoing but unheralded tradition of fine Philadelphia third basemen. Since the start of the All-Star tradition in 1933, the Phils have fielded 27 different third basemen. Seven of them, or more than 25 percent of all Phillie third basemen, (Pinky Whitney, Pinky May, Willie Jones, Dick Allen, Mike Schmidt, Dave Hollins, and Scott Rolen) have earned All-Star status.

In 1992, Headley blossomed. In his first full season, he was second in the NL in runs scored with 104. He was tied for fourth in homers with 27. He placed eighth in total bases with 275 and tenth in walks with 76. Headly also worked pitchers intelligently and developed into an aggressive leader on an aggressive team.

"I'm never going to charge after a pitcher again. It hurts our team when I get suspended. What I am going to do is this. If a pitcher throws at me and you don't go after one of their guys the next inning, then I'm coming after you when we get into the clubhouse."

[DAVE HOLLINS—FORMER PHILLIES THIRD BASEMAN]

"Headley did the most amazing thing I've ever seen in a clubhouse," Curt Schilling recalls. "He charged the mound in Chicago after he was hit by a pitch for the second time in the game. He ended up suspended for four games and our team took a nosedive while he was gone. When he came back,

batting in winter ball, the Phils grabbed him in the Rule 5 draft in December. He appeared in 72 games as a Phil in 1990 and managed only a .184 average. In 1991, he started the season at AAA Scranton,

Right: Dave Hollins continued the tradition of fine Philadelphia third basemen in the early 1990s.
Otto Greule Jr./Getty Images

> ## "It was like I had Phillies withdrawal problems. Our '93 team was so close and so intense, I never found the same atmosphere and spirit in any other clubhouse. I never again experienced that intense desire to win every game. I think not having that feeling hurt my performance."
>
> [DAVE HOLLINS—FORMER PHILLIES THIRD BASEMAN]

he gathered the pitchers up in the clubhouse and told us, 'I'm never going to charge after a pitcher again. It hurts our team when I get suspended. What I *am* going to do is this. If a pitcher throws at me and you *don't* go after one of their guys the next inning, then I'm coming after *you* when we get into the clubhouse.' He was serious. Head is the only guy I've ever played with that I believe is capable of annihilating someone on the field! He also assured us that, if anyone charged one of us on the mound, there was no way they could get to us before he got to them. He was right. I felt totally safe with him over there at third. It helped me start to take charge of home plate and made me a tougher pitcher."

Dave made the All-Star team that toured Japan after the '92 season. The following year, his stats were practically identical to 1992. Again he scored 104 runs and drove in 93. His homers dipped to 18 but his walks increased to 85. He played in his first and only mid-summer classic that season, joining teammates John Kruk, Darren Daulton, and Terry Mulholland.

Unfortunately, after the '93 season, Dave never regained his All-Star form. He was plagued with injuries the rest of his career. He was traded to Boston from the Phils in 1995. Afterwards he bounced around between Minnesota, Seattle, Anaheim, and Toronto.

"I had injuries and when I was traded away, I just never enjoyed the game and camaraderie as much," Dave confesses. "It was like I had Phillies withdrawal problems. Our '93 team was so close and so intense, I never found the same atmosphere and spirit in any other clubhouse. I never again experienced that intense desire to win every game. I think not having that feeling hurt my performance."

Manager Larry Bowa sensed a lack of focus and intensity in the Phillies' 2001 clubhouse. He believed that having Head around his young charges would help infuse some much-needed fire. He invited Dave Hollins to come down to Florida in 2002. After spring training, Dave came back up north as a member of the squad. He ended his major league career that season as a Phil.

"I was glad to have the opportunity to come back," Dave says. "I was too intense when I was a younger player in the early '90s. I was unseasoned and immature, and my response was aggressiveness. It's not really the way I am. I'm glad I got back here and had a chance to show people the real me."

Right: Nicknamed "Headly," Dave Hollins led the Phillies as much with his intensity as with his bat.
Courtesy of the Philadelphia Phillies

PETE INCAVIGLIA

Pete Incaviglia, or Inky as he is known, spent only a few seasons in Philadelphia. One of those seasons was 1993, the "Phillies' Enchanted Season" as longtime Philly writer Bill Lyon dubbed it. The Phils won a flag that year. They staged a dramatic, unexpected last place-to-first place rebound that charmed the city forevermore. Inky's Bunyanesque contributions to that '93 season solidified his spot in local lore and made him a fan favorite. The love was mutual.

"I'll always consider myself a Phillie," Inky confesses. "I played a number of years in Texas. I can't say anything but good things about the people in Texas. They're terrific. But Philly fans—they're a whole 'nother thing. More than anything else, though, it was the guys I played with in Philly. It was the organization here, the Phillies family. I never enjoyed baseball as much as I did that year. The game never felt the same to me after that season with that particular group of guys. I went through kind of a Phillies withdrawal problem after I left Philly—same as Dave Hollins and a few others."

Inky found identity in the wacky 1993 Phils clubhouse filled with free-spirited, mulleted, pie-tossing gypsies, tramps, and thieves. Inky was the

Born: April 2, 1964, Pebble Beach, California
Position: Outfield
Years with the Phillies: 1993, 1994, 1996
Uniform Numbers: 9, 22
Major League Stats: .246, 206 HR, 655 RBI
Post Season Stats: .167, 1 HR, 1 RBI; 1993
World Series: .125, 0 HR, 1 RBI
Honors:
- California State Player of the Year three times
- College Player of the Year in 1985
- Topps 1985 All-Rookie Team

bruiser of the group, the burly enforcer—an image he savored and the fans loved.

"Inky is kind of like the guy who grew up in the mob but decided to play baseball instead," Curt Schilling jokes. "He was a strong presence and kind of typified our team. He loved to play the game and was deadly serious on the field. Off the field, he was always up for a good time."

"Are you kidding? With a name like Incaviglia, those Italian South Philly fans loved me!" Inky chuckles. "Actually, it's not that easy with the fans. Gaining their respect is anything but automatic. You need to earn it. You'd better play all-out all the time or those fans will be all over you. That's the only way I know how to play this game—all-out. Some guys can't handle the fan

Left: Pete Incaviglia's 24 home runs and 89 RBIs in a part-time role were key to the 1993 Phillies' success.
Jonathan Daniel/Getty Images

pressure in this town. It helped me. It helped our whole team."

Inky didn't burst into prominence out of nowhere. He was the California State Player of the Year *three times* at Monterey High School. He followed up on his high school success with an outstanding college career. He set NCAA marks by slamming a hundred career home runs and recording a .951 slugging percentage at Oklahoma State. In 1985, he was honored as College Player of the Year after setting NCAA records for home runs (48), total bases (285), and slugging percentage (1.140) over the 75-game collegiate schedule.

Incaviglia was Montreal's first-round pick (and eighth selection overall) in the June 1985 draft. That November, the Expos traded their young prospect to Texas for Bob Sebra and Jim Anderson. Inky was on the major-league fast track. In 1986, he became just the fifth non-pitcher and 14th player since the draft was initiated in 1965 to go directly to the major leagues. Inky broke in spectacularly. The burly rookie led his team, the Texas Rangers, in home runs with 30 and RBIs with 88. He continued to pound the ball year after year. He eventually became the first Ranger in the history of the franchise to hit 20 or more homers in five consecutive seasons.

On April 7, 1991, Detroit inked Inky as a free agent. When he left the Lone Star State, he ranked third on the Rangers' all-time home run list behind Frank Howard and Larry Parrish. He also ranked ninth on the club's all-time RBI list.

Bad fortune followed Inky to Motown. He walloped only 11 home runs and drove in only 38. Injuries hampered his performance. He missed almost a month with a chest wall strain. No sooner had he recovered from that when he sprained a wrist and missed three weeks of action.

He was shipped off to Houston after the season and had a subpar year with the Astros. The Phils picked him up as a free agent on December 8, 1992.

Pete split time with Milt Thompson in left field in '93. He socked 24 homers and drove in 89 as a part-time performer. His batting average was a career-high .274.

> ## "Inky's leadership was a key to our success. Here was a guy with fire in his belly. Inky wanted to play every day but he sucked it up. He knew that platooning was the only way the '93 Phils were going to win."
>
> [DARREN DAULTON—FORMER PHILLIES CATCHER]

"Inky's leadership was a key to our success," Darren Daulton acknowledges. "Here was a guy with fire in his belly. Inky wanted to play every day but he sucked it up. He knew that platooning was the only way the '93 Phils were going to win. He was having a big season personally and he was forced to sit down a lot of times when he was on a tear. But we had lots of guys contributing that season [eight Phils hit ten or more homers in '93: Inky, Darren Daulton, Lenny Dykstra, Dave Hollins, John

Kruk, Wes Chamberlain, and Mariano Duncan]. Inky's attitude and acceptance at being platooned was a strong message to the younger guys. The team was more important than the individual."

Inky was capable of some monstrous hot streaks. Only three Phils in the club's long history have homered in four consecutive games more than once. Schmidt did it ten times. Jim Thome and Inky both did it twice. Six times in his three years as a Phil, Inky hit two homers in a game, a mark that earns him the 12th slot on the club's all-time list for most times hitting two homers in a game.

Inky's blasts were Herculean. He hit team- and crowd-pumping, tape-measure bombs. The most celebrated came against the Braves in Game 1 of the 1993 National League Championship Series. At that point, the Phils had been using IBM to measure home run distances for two seasons. Inky's 423-foot smash to dead center topped the list of 258 homers hit since the system was installed. Ironically, the very next game, the Braves' Fred McGriff usurped Inky's top spot with a monster shot to right field.

Unfortunately, injuries besieged Pete after the Enchanted Season. He played in only 80 games in 1994 and belted only 13 round-trippers. He was granted free agency after 1994 and signed with the Chiba Lotte Marlins in the Japan Pacific League. He returned to Philly in '96, crushing 16 homers in 269 at-bats before being dealt to Baltimore with Todd Zeile for pitchers Calvin Maduro and Garrett Stephenson. Inky spent 1997 and 1998 languishing around with the Orioles, Yankees, Tigers, and Astros. He tried a few comebacks after his final season in 1998 but never latched on.

Today, Pete Incaviglia resides in Texas. He returned to the Delaware Valley briefly in 2002 to join the coaching staff of the Atlantic City Surf, when his '93 sidekick Mitch Williams was the manager.

Above: Power was the name of Pete Incaviglia's game. He totaled 206 home runs during his major-league career, including a 423-foot shot to dead center field against the Braves in the 1993 NLCS.
Jonathan Daniel/Getty Images

HARRY KALAS

Way down in the state of North Carolina, surrounded by mountains far removed from Philly's concrete and macadam plains, Quaker City expatriate Chuck Brodsky fusses with a hissy old radio. He's trying to tune in the Phillies game. Chuck Brodsky is a globe-trotting folksinger who hails from the Philly 'burbs.

"I grew up listening to the Phillies," Chuck explains. "Doesn't matter where I live, I'll always be a Phillies fan first. I'm always trying to catch the Phils game on TV or radio. I'm not alone. It doesn't matter where I go. I run into rabid Phillie fans every place I give a concert."

One of the songs those Phillie fans demand at a Brodsky concert is his ode to the Phillies' long-time announcing tandem of Richie Ashburn and Harry Kalas. Brodsky composed the song *"Whitey and Harry"* after Richie Ashburn's death. Here's an excerpt (for the complete song lyrics, or to order a copy, check out www.chuckbrodsky.com).

Moonlight on the mountains
North Carolina two-lane
Trying to find a ballgame
No matter how bad the reception
Whitey, man, I miss you
When I listen to the Phillies
And there's Harry going on without you
Harry … good old Harry

Left: The voice of Harry Kalas has been a mainstay for Philadelphia fans since 1971.
Courtesy of the Philadelphia Phillies

Whitey and Harry teamed up on Phils' broadcasts from 1971 to 1997. The whole town adopted several of their pet expressions. Kalas invented Philly pop phrases like *"Outta here"* and *"Watch that baby."* Ashburn chipped in with *"Oh brother,"* and *"Hard to believe, Harry."*

Ashburn hailed from Nebraska. Kalas grew up near Chicago. The two Midwesterners clicked together. Both were easygoing. Both exuded hopeful optimism borne of Phillie love and loyalty.

"I was sold on baseball because of a guy who hailed from around these parts [the Delaware Valley]," Harry Kalas reminisces. "The first game I ever went to was in Chicago. Mickey Vernon was in the visitor's dugout on a rainy Chicago afternoon. I went down to the dugout and kind of peeked in. Mickey saw me and beckoned me in. There I was—a starry-eyed kid *inside* a real major league dugout. That day, I set my sights on spending the rest of my life in or around baseball."

Harry didn't have enough talent to play the game professionally. He wound up announcing games at the University of Iowa. After graduation, Harry was drafted into the Army and assigned to Hawaii. "Tough duty, but somebody had to get the assignment," Harry chuckles. While in Hawaii, Harry started doing interviews and profiles of fellow servicemen for the army radio station. Soon he was hired by KGU radio to broadcast for the Hawaii Islanders of the Pacific Coast League. Harry learned to be innovative on that gig.

> **"The first game I ever went to was in Chicago. Mickey Vernon was in the visitor's dugout on a rainy Chicago afternoon. I went down to the dugout and kind of peeked in. Mickey saw me and beckoned me in. There I was, a starry-eyed kid *inside* a real major league dugout. That day, I set my sights on spending the rest of my life in or around baseball."**
>
> [HARRY KALAS—PHILLIES BROADCASTER]

"When we played away games in the U.S., I stayed back in Hawaii," Harry reconstructs. "We didn't broadcast those games live. First we got a tickertape account of the game. It said what each batter did, but it didn't account for each pitch. I had to 'invent' the at-bat itself. I also had to come up with some sound effects. When a guy got a hit, I'd tap a pencil against a box. We'd inject canned crowd noise into the broadcast too. It sounded like we were playing in Yankee Stadium. Of course, it was up to us to pace the game. That can be dangerous, given all that Hawaii has to offer in evening entertainment! When we wanted to get out of the studio early, we had every batter swinging and hitting the first pitch, or striking out on three pitches, or walking on four. The game would be played in record time."

While Harry was in Hawaii, the offer he had dreamed about since that day in the dugout with Mickey Vernon came in. The expansion team, the Houston Colt 45s, hired him as announcer. Harry remained in Houston for a six years. There he made the acquaintance of Bill Giles, Houston's young PR guy. When Giles trekked to Philadelphia, he offered Harry Kalas a broadcasting job with the Phils. Harry would replace Bill Campbell, a Phillies broadcaster since 1962. Harry accepted and the rest, as they say, is history.

Philadelphia first met Harry Kalas when he donned a tuxedo to emcee the opening ceremonies at Veterans Stadium. Thirty-two years later, Kalas reprised his emcee role at the Vet's closing ceremonies. In the three-decade interim, Harry Kalas's voice became one of sport's most recognizable.

Over his years in Philadelphia, Harry has broadcast Big Five basketball and Notre Dame football. He voices over several programs for NFL Films.

Kalas has been the recipient of numerous honors as a broadcaster. He won the 2002 Board of Governors Award at the Mid-Atlantic Emmy Awards and the Lifetime Achievement Award from the Philadelphia Sports Congress. His greatest honor to date has been his selection as the 2002 winner of the National Baseball Hall of Fame and Museum's Ford C. Frick Award. The award is bestowed on broadcasters who have "made major contributions to baseball." Harry Kalas also received the inaugural Legacy of Excellence Award from the Philadelphia Sports Hall of Fame on February 9, 2004. Harry was one of 19 inducted into the Philadelphia's first sport Hall of Fame class.

Right: Harry Kalas is greeted by the Phillie Phanatic in June, 2002, a month before his induction into the broadcasters' wing of the National Baseball Hall of Fame.
AP/WWP

JIM KONSTANTY

The names Ashburn, Roberts, Simmons, Ennis, and Sisler seem the most immortalized of the Whiz Kids. But the guy who was most acknowledged at the time was Jim Konstanty. Konstanty was a quiet, bespectacled reliever whose celebrity has not weathered so well as that of some of his teammates. The Phils picked up Konstanty from Cincinnati in 1949. He put up respectable numbers—9-5, 3.25 ERA—in his Phillie debut season.

In 1950, however, Konstanty was phenomenal. Despite the yeoman efforts of staff-mate Robin Roberts—who was 20-11 in 1950—and Del Ennis—who batted .313, slammed 30 homers, and drove in a league-leading 126 runs—Jim Konstanty was selected the National League MVP. Steve Carlton, Steve Bedrosian, and John Denny have all won Cy Young Awards as Phillies. Jim Konstanty is the only Phillies hurler *ever* to win an MVP.

"That MVP award *had* to go to a Phillie in 1950," Maje McDonnell, coach of the 1950 Whiz Kids asserts. "We had some guys who had great seasons. But Konstanty was *the* guy that year, no doubt about it. He was there every time we needed a win. You know, baseball wasn't the same then. We didn't have long and short relievers and setup men and

Born: March 21, 1917, Strykersville, New York
Died: June 11, 1976, Oneonta, New York
Position: Relief Pitcher
Years with the Phillies: 1948-1954
Uniform Number: 35
Major League Stats: 66-48, 3.46 ERA
Phillies Playoffs Stats: 0-1, 2.40 ERA
Honors:
• 1950 National League MVP
• 1950 UPI NL Player of the Year
• 1950 *Sporting News* Pitcher of the Year
• 1950 Associated Press Male Athlete of the Year Award
• 1950 NL All-Star
• RH Relief pitcher, Phillies All-Centennial Team

closers like we have now. Konstanty was amazingly versatile. He pitched 152 innings that season. Closers today don't even pitch 100 innings. [Manager] Eddie Sawyer would put Konstanty into some games as early as the fourth or fifth inning. Sawyer put him in one game in the second inning and Jim finished the game. Jim started the World Series for us, you know. He pitched a helluva game, too, and lost 1-0. Konstanty could give us anything we needed that year. We wouldn't have won that pennant if he hadn't had such a great season."

Right: Perhaps the least remembered hero of the 1950s "Whiz Kids," reliever Jim Konstanty was named the 1950 National League MVP.
Courtesy of the Philadelphia Phillies

> **"Not only did Jim Konstanty play a huge role as a reliever, but he was also a steadying influence on the younger guys. He had the experience that the rest of us lacked at that point in our careers."**
>
> [ROBIN ROBERTS—HALL OF FAME PHILLIES PITCHER]

Robin Roberts concurs: "We were mostly a group of young guys just coming into our own. Not only did Jim Konstanty play a huge role as a reliever, but he was also a steadying influence on the younger guys. He had the experience that the rest of us lacked at that point in our careers."

That's a strange role for Phillie relievers, given the roll call of wild, wooly, and wacky seventies-eighties-nineties relief specialists like Tug McGraw, Steve Bedrosian, Al Holland, Rickie Botallico, and Larry Andersen.

"Jim was a straight shooter," Maje McDonnell explains. "He didn't drink, smoke, or curse. He had unshakable confidence. That was his greatest asset. Konstanty fully believed no one could hit him. That year he was right."

Konstanty dropped off precipitously to 4-11 in 1951. He climbed back on to the winning track the following season with a 5-3 record. Then in '53, the Phils converted him into a starter. Big Jim rewarded them with a hardy impressive 14-10 season.

"Eddie Sawyer is the guy who made Jim a reliever," Maje McDonnell analyzes. "Eddie was a bright man. He graduated cum laude from Ithaca. He always told me, 'Maje, Konstanty is just a two-year pitcher.'

Eddie meant that Jim could fool major leaguers for about two years. Then they'd catch up with him. You see, Konstanty threw different than anyone else in the league. He only threw two pitches: a palm ball and a slider. The palm ball would tail away from a left-handed batter and the slider tailed away from a rightie. Jim didn't have much velocity. Sawyer was right. The batters did catch up to Konstanty, but not till he fooled them for a couple of years."

"I think Jim was a school-teacher back in Syracuse," Robin Roberts recalls. "He played basketball there, too. He was a dedicated athlete. He watched his diet, didn't drink beer, and worked out every day."

Jim Konstanty manned the mound in Philly from 1948 through 1954. Duing that stretch, he won 51 games for the Phils and lost only 39. At season's end in '54, he was traded to the Yankees to help the Bronx Bombers in their stretch run. The Yanks didn't catch up to the Indians that year. The Tribe won 111 games, while the Yanks won *only* 103 to finish a distant eight games back. Konstanty made his brief presence felt. He was 1-1 with a glittery 0.98 ERA and two saves. In '55, Konstanty fooled the American Leaguers again. He went 7-2 as a Yank. His 2.32 ERA in 73-2/3 innings of work was the best on the staff.

In 1956, Jim pitched only 11 innings for New York before being dealt to the Cardinals. Konstanty pitched 39-1/3 innings for St. Louis in '56. He was 1-1 with a 4.58 ERA. After that season, he called it quits.

Jim passed away on June 11, 1976 in Oneonta New York near Strykersville, the town of his birth. He was nine months shy of his 60th birthday when he died.

Right: Coming out of the bullpen, Jim Konstanty totaled 152 innings in 1950.
Courtesy of the Philadelphia Athletics Historical Society

MIKE LIEBERTHAL

As of 2004, Mike Lieberthal was the dean of current Philly athletes. Lieby has played longer for a Philadelphia professional team than any of his Philadelphia peers.

Lieby was the Phils' first pick (and third overall) in the June, 1990 draft. He's been with the Phillies' organization ever since. Mike reported to Martinsville after he was drafted. The following year he split his time between Spartansburg and Clearwater.

"When Lieby came to Clearwater, it went a long way toward improving our program," John Timberlake (no relation to Justin) recalls. "We hadn't had much success till then, but you could tell that this was a guy destined for the big leagues. Lieby was a cut above."

Lieby was off to AA Reading in 1992 where he won the Paul Owens Award as the best player in the Phils' minor league system. He played at Scranton the entire '92 season. He was in Scranton again in 1993 when he was first brought up to the parent club in 1994. He started the '95 season with the Phils but was optioned to Scranton in mid-May for a brief tour. By August 26, he was back in Philly for good to replace the injured Darren Daulton.

Born: January 18, 1972, Glendale, California
Position: Catcher
Years with the Phillies: 1994-Current
Uniform Number: 24
Major League Stats (up to 2004): .277, 112 HR, 465 RBI
Honors:
• 2002 NL Comeback Player of the Year (*Sporting News* and Player's Choice)
• 1999 NL Player of the Week May 17-23
• 1999 Rawlings Gold Glove winner
• 1992 Paul Owens Award presented annually to the top minor league player in the Phils system
• 2000 Chairman for the Corporate Alliance for Drug Education fundraising drive.

Lieby carried a .277 lifetime average into the 2004 season. Twice (1999, 2003) Mike has ended the season on the plus side of .300. His best season so far was 1999 when he batted .300 and slugged 31 homers to eclipse Darren Daulton's 1992 Phillies mark of 27. Old-timers might remember that catcher Stan Lopata hit 32 round-trippers in 1956. However Stosh hit only 26 of them as a catcher.

The 21 road homers Lieby smacked in '99 were the fourth highest total in club history. He became only the fourth catcher in major league history to hit

Left: The Phillies' first pick in the 1990 draft, Mike Lieberthal has been the team's starting catcher since 1997.
Jon Adams/Icon SMI

.300 and pound 30 homers in the same season. He was also the first Phillie to perform that feat in a complete season since Greg Luzinski (.309, 39) accomplished it in 1977.

Lieby was picked for the All-Star team that season. He also earned his first Gold Glove, becoming the only Phillie catcher other than Bob Boone ever to be so honored. Mike had a 100-game errorless streak that season. He finished with a glittery .997 fielding percentage, which eclipsed the .994 club standard set by Spud Davis back in 1931 (the Phillies' 1931 pitching staff had the NL's worst ERA. Perhaps Spud wasn't that great defensively—not many pitches actually made it all the way into his glove.)

Mike rebounded in 2002 when he hit .279 with 15 homers. His performance earned him *The Sporting News's* Comeback Player of the Year Award. He shared the Players Choice Comeback Player of the Year Award with John Smoltz.

In 2003, Lieby tied Darren Daulton's club record of seven consecutive opening-day starts at catcher. He barely missed becoming the second Philllie backstop ever to finish in the NL's top ten hitters. Spud Davis accomplished that feat in 1932 and again in 1933. Lieby's lofty .313 average placed him 12th among National League batsmen.

"Nobody works harder than Mike," Jim Thome observes. "He's a quiet guy but a good role model for the younger players. He has a strict exercise routine

"Nobody works harder than Mike. He's a quiet guy but a good role model for the younger players. He has a strict exercise routine that he's faithful to. And he's always in the batting cage."

[JIM THOME—PHILLIES FIRST BASEMAN]

Though injuries diminished his batting average and power output in 2000, Lieby was selected to his second consecutive All-Star game. In the game, Mike went 1-2 and scored a run. In the second half of the season, Lieby missed more than two weeks of action after he sprained his ankle in a collision at home plate with the Yankees' Bernie Williams.

Lieberthal succumbed to injury again in 2001 when he played only 34 games. He tore his ACL, MCL, and lateral meniscus diving back to first base on a pickoff attempt. The injury necessitated mid-June, season-ending knee surgery.

that he's faithful to. And he's always in the batting cage."

Mike nurtured that regimen as a kid. He grew up in Glendale, California. His father installed a batting cage in their yard so Mike could work on his game.

"Lieby never stops working on his game," Dan Stephenson says. "He was the first guy who ever came in and took videos of opposing teams' games

Right: In 1999, Mike Lieberthal earned his first Gold Glove, the only Phillies catcher other than Bob Boone ever so honored. He had a 100-game errorless streak that year, and a .997 fielding percentage overall.
Drew Hallowell/Icon SMI

home. Tom Glavine of the Mets has an approach to pitching that's similar to Randy Wolf's. So Lieby watches the tapes of Mets games that Glavine pitches. He'll study how Tom Glavine pitches the Marlins' hitters or whatever other team Wolfie is due to pitch against."

"Lieby made me a believer," Curt Schilling says. "Back in 1995, when Darren Daulton was physically unable to catch anymore, we picked up Benito Santiago. Benito had an awesome year for us in '96. I felt we needed him in order to succeed in 1997. I made that fact known to everyone. We didn't get Benito. He went off to Toronto in '97, so Lieby played his first full year as the starter. He proved himself to me and everyone else. It was obvious we had a quality catcher who understood the complexities of pitching. I bought him a Rolex at the end of the year in recognition of the way he handled the game when I was on the mound."

Right: Mike Lieberthal became only the fourth catcher in major league history to hit .300 with 30 home runs in the same season in 1999.
Ed Wolfstein/Icon SMI

ART MAHAFFEY

"For a right hander, Art Mahaffey had the best move to first base I've ever seen," John Callison recalls. "You couldn't read him at all. And he got the ball over there in a hurry, too."

"Before I came up to the majors, I predicted I'd pick off the first two guys who reached first base on me," Art Mahaffey smiles. "I stuck to my prediction."

Art Mahaffey broke into the big leagues in style. Art was inserted into a game against the St. Louis Cardinals in relief on July 30, 1960. Curt Flood, the first major-league batter he ever faced, reached first base. Mahaffey promptly picked him off. The next batter, Bill White, also reached first. Mahaffey nabbed him as well. Mahaffey closed out the inning by fanning the next guy for the third out.

Art Mahaffey went on to fan lots of batters in a brief career. He ranks eighth on the Phillies' all-time list for most 10-strikeout games. He twirled six such gems, one less than the No. 7 guy on the list, Robin Roberts. Art fanned more opponents in a nine-inning game than any other Phillie hurler in history. He struck out 17 Cubs on April 23, 1961. Chris Short surpassed him for most Ks in one game when he whiffed 18 Mets in 1965. But he did it in 15 innings.

Left: Art Mahaffey's star flickered brightly, if briefly, for the Phils in the early '60s. He made the All-Star team twice and struck out 10-plus batters in a game six times.
Courtesy of the Philadelphia Phillies

> **Born:** June 4, 1938, Cincinnati, Ohio
> **Position:** Pitcher
> **Years with the Phillies:** 1960-1965
> **Uniform Number:** 28
> **Major League Stats:** 59-64, 4.17 ERA
> **Honors:**
> • Picked for the National League All-Star team in 1961 and 1962

"I pitched eight and two-thirds innings in a game in 1964," Mahaffey relates. "Gene Mauch yanked me after a bloop hit to right. The reliever got the next guy out and I got the win, 2-1. The next day, Ray Kelly, Stan Hochman, and some other beat writers were hanging around the clubhouse. I walked in and nobody said a word. Finally I said, 'Hey, how come you guys didn't say 'Good game' to me? I won last night.' They told me, 'You didn't really win. You didn't finish!' That mind set sure has changed. Nowadays you get a 'quality start' if you pitch *five innings*. Back then, you got no respect if you couldn't finish your own game."

That policy—completing the games you started—exacted a price. Unfortunately, Art Mahaffey, like other pitchers in his era, worked his arm too hard.

"They didn't keep pitch counts in the sixties," Mahaffey reflects. "We had to pitch and keep pitching. Otherwise we got sent down to the minors. That was the rule. I pitched when I was in so much pain I couldn't lift my arm."

Mahaffey made the All-Star team in both 1961 and 1962. Speaking of complete games, in 1961, Mahaffey finished fifth among NL hurlers in complete games. In 1962, he tied Warren Spahn and Billy O'Dell for the NL lead in the category.

"Things were so different then," Mahaffey confides. "We didn't get proper advice on how to train. Baseball people were so far off base on what was good and what was bad for your body. For instance, we were advised not to lift any more weight than three pounds. Baseball people thought that working out with weights would ruin a pitcher's arm.

a graduate of the Mayo Clinic and knew what he was doing. He worked the knots out of my arm. No one else could. Once he was gone, all I did was pitch with the pain."

Art hurt his arm early in the 1962 season, and never fully recovered.

"I was pitching in 40-degree weather on one of those cold April nights," he explains. "I won 2-1 and pitched nine innings. But that was the start of my trouble. After pitching that night, I started seven of the next 20 games, and my arm got progressively worse."

Mahaffey starred during a bleak era for the Phillies.

"They didn't keep pitch counts in the sixties. We had to pitch and keep pitching. Otherwise we got sent down to the minors. That was the rule. I pitched when I was in so much pain I couldn't lift my arm."

[ART MAHAFFEY—FORMER PHILLIES PITCHER]

They thought the arm would pull out of the shoulder socket or something. Steve Carlton changed that kind of thinking. Lefty was a pioneer in bringing weight training into the game. I've worked out on the Nautilus machine for years now. There was no Nautilus in my playing days. If there were, I might have pitched 15 more years.

"We didn't even have a pitching coach when I came up. As for trainers, Frank Wiechek was on the staff when I first came up, but he was replaced. Frank was the only one who knew how to make my arm feel okay so I could pitch without pain. He was

"In my rookie year, we lost 23 games in a row," Mahaffey laughs. "I lost 10 straight games that year and wound up 11-19 for the year. [Pitcher] Johnny Buzhardt broke the losing streak. After he did, I pitched a one-hit shutout and three-hit shutout in my next two starts."

Then came 1964. Mahaffey appeared in two key games in the midst of the Phils' infamous 10-game September, pennant-losing streak.

"I started that streak off," Art reflects. "I was pitching against the Reds. They had a great team— Vada Pinson, Pete Rose, Deron Johnson, Tommy

Harper and others. I lost 1-0 when a rookie named Chico Ruiz stole home while Frank Robinson was batting. There's one of the greatest clutch hitters in the history of the game at the plate, and this rookie steals home. I also pitched the sixth game in that losing streak. I went out of the game when we were leading the Braves. Bobby Shantz relieved me and Rico Carty hit a triple to win the game."

A long-standing dirge in Philly has it that the Phils folded because manager Gene Mauch panicked. Mauch pitched only Chris Short and Jim Bunning during the losing streak despite having fresher arms available.

"I don't say much about Gene any more," Art confesses. "Everyone knows he and I didn't see eye to eye. Those things happened a long time ago, and it's over now. But yeah, I could have pitched. I had lots of arm trouble, but my arm was okay at that point."

The numbers bear testament to Art's assertion. The Phils' pitching staff was not just a two-man show in '64. Neither Bunning nor Short won 20. Bunning won 19, Short 17. The rest of the staff chalked up a lot of Ws too. Mahaffey and Dennis Bennett each won 12, while Ray Culp chipped in with eight.

Arm troubles caught up with Art in '65. He worked only 71 innings in forging a 2-5 record. He was traded to St. Louis the following year.

"I didn't have much luck in St. Louis," Art confesses. "I lost a 3-1 game against Juan Marichal. Then I lost two straight to Jim Maloney. He struck out 15 in the first game, and 16 in the next. I was 1-3 after four games and never started again."

Art hung up the spikes after one year in St. Louis.

"I've been in the insurance business for 30 years now," Art states with pride. "I did some PR work as a player and spent three years as a stock broker. I'm in good shape. I work out religiously. I had a good career in baseball and a fine career afterwards."

Above: Art Mahaffey appeared in two games during the Phillies' infamous 10-game losing streak in September 1964.
Brace Photo

GARY MATTHEWS

D an Stephenson heads the Phillies video department. Ask him about Gary Matthews and he chuckles "When The Sarge sees me wearing my '83 pennant ring, he always says the same thing, 'Hey Video, I see you're wearing my ring.'"

The Sarge (more on that nickname later) is Gary Matthews, star Phillie outfielder of the early '80s. The Sarge has some justification for his claim as '83's lord of the rings. He was a wrecking crew in the 1983 NLCS when the Phils beat the Dodgers. He was *not* a one-man wrecking crew, although a lot of fans remember it that way. That fact in itself is a tribute to his brilliance in that particular series. It's not often that history effaces the exploits of a Hall of Famer. Sarge's teammate Mike Schmidt hit a torrid .467 in that same series. Throw in his walks and Schmidt reached base in more than half his plate appearances. However, most fans don't remember Schmidt in that series. They remember Sarge.

Gary Matthews hit .429 with three homers to cop the '83 NLCS MVP. The Phils doubled the Dodgers in runs scored in a four-game best-of-five series. Schmidt homered off Jerry Reuss in the first inning of the opener, providing the margin for a 1-0

Born: July 5, 1950, San Francisco, California
Position: Outfield
Years with the Phillies: 1981-1983
Uniform Number: 34
Major League Stats: .281, 234 HR, 978 RBI
Phillies Postseason Stats: 1981 Division Playoff, .400, 1 HR, 1 RBI; 1983 NLCS, .429, 3 HR, 8 RBI; 1983 World Series, .250, 1 HR, 1 RBI
Honors: 1979 Atlanta Braves All-Star

Phillie victory. Sarge took over from there. In Game 2, he reenacted Schmidt's Game 1 thunder. Sarge's homer off Fernando Valenzuela was the Phils' only score in a 4-1 loss. In games three and four, played in Philly, Sarge pounded four hits. The Phils won each game 7-2 to earn a trip to the World Series. Sarge slammed a homer in each game and drove in half of the Phils' fourteen runs.

"Dusty Baker killed us in the '77 NLCS," Dan Stephenson recalls. "If you remember, he hit a grand slam in the second game off Jim Lonborg. Then he hit that homer off Lefty in the pouring rain at the Vet to clinch the series. Well, after the '83 NLCS, it was kind of neat. Dusty Baker and Sarge were boyhood friends. They grew up together. After Sarge's great performance in '83, Dusty was the first one over to the clubhouse to congratulate him."

Left: Gary Matthews is best remembered by Phillies fans for his MVP performance in the 1983 NLCS.
Courtesy of the Philadelphia Phillies

"Sarge was the hardest working outfielder I ever saw. He came to play and he came to win every day. He was an intense competitor. But outside the lines he was like the rest of that '83 team... Sarge was in the middle of all the fun. He never stopped needling everybody in the locker room. He was a positive personality to have around the clubhouse."

[AL HOLLAND—FORMER PHILLIES CLOSER]

Sarge had picked the right stage to shine. The Quaker City was stoked about winning the '83 pennant, and the Sarge was an instant hero.

"'I love this town. I haven't paid for anything in months!' That's what Sarge told me after that NLCS," Dan Stephenson continues. "Sarge savored the reception Philly gave him after the '83 NLCS. I'll tell you a funny story. I had a couple tickets to the Flyers game one night. Sarge knew nothing about hockey but he decided to go with me for kicks. Sarge used to dress to the nines. He was wearing a fur coat and a cool hat. We were walking along the terrace at the old Spectrum before the game. People saw him strutting toward them and parted in front of us. They were yelling things like, 'Great series, Sarge!' Eventually Sarge turns to me and says, 'I *like* this place. Hockey is *fine!*'

"Then we were sitting in our seats and Bobby Clarke gets introduced. The place goes wild. Sarge asks me, 'Who's that?' I say. 'It's Clarkey. The fans go crazy when they announce his name.' Sarge shoots back, 'Just like the Sarge!' with this big smile on his face."

"Gary was a popular player," Larry Shenk remembers. "He's had a good post-baseball career too because of his personality. He's been a hitting coach and broadcaster. As a player, he was one of the few guys who ever went out to his position and made a show of acknowledging the fans in left field. Sarge loved the spectacle and he loved the Philly crowd. They loved him back."

"They sure did," echoes Ruben Amaro, current Phillies Assistant GM and former Phillies player. "When I was a batboy for the Phils, Sarge was a treat. He'd get all fired up before a game. Before he took the field, he'd yell to me, 'OK, kid. It's *showtime!*'

As for that name—Sarge—Pete Rose came up with it.

"One day Pete yelled over to him, 'Hey Sarge,'" Larry Christenson recalls. "Gary answered, 'Why you calling me that?' Rose said, 'Because you take command. You step up like a Sargent.' Gary chewed on it for a minute and said, 'Yeah, I like that.' That was basically it. Gary was Sarge from then on."

Right: Gary Matthews takes a swing during the 1983 World Series against Baltimore. Matthews's .429 average in the NLCS carried the Phillies to the Series.
Focus on Sport/Getty Images

Sarge gave some good years to the Phils. He arrived in Philadelphia via Atlanta for Bob Walk in 1981. Walk was popular in Philly. Walk was a rookie during the '80 World Championship season. He had an 11-7 record that season and was the surprise starter of game one in the World Series.

The Sarge, an Atlanta All-Star in 1979, batted .301 his first year as a Phil in '81. His all-out play made him an immediate favorite in the Quaker City. He hammered a respectable nine homers in the strike-shortened season. He also slammed a team-leading 21 doubles. But it was the other facets of his play that impressed the Phillie crowd. Sarge chugged the basepaths like a runaway train, swiped 15 bases, dismantled double-play attempts, and gobbled up extra bases at every opportunity. He made a habit of running out from under his cap.

> "Sarge is one of those guys who left a big mark on the organization. He was unique—a fun guy with a huge personality. He had his own style in everything."
>
> [DAN STEPHENSON—PHILLIES VIDEO DIRECTOR]

"Yeah," Ruben Amaro adds drolly. "He did that so the batboy—me—had to hustle out, retrieve it, and run it over to him."

In '82, Sarge's average slipped to a still-respectable .281. He socked 19 homers and knocked in 83 runs, while scoring 89 himself. He doubled a team-best 31 times, and pilfered 21 bases, which was second-best on the squad.

In '83, Sarge had an off year. He batted only .258 and socked only 10 homers. But he certainly came through in the postseason.

In '84, he was traded to the Cubs along with Bob Dernier and reliever Porfi Altamirano. Mike Diaz and Bill Campbell became Phils.

Sarge responded with a good season in Cubland. He batted .291 with 14 homers and 82 RBIs to help the Cubs run away to a divisional flag. The Cubbies finished six and a half games ahead of the runner-up Mets. Besides Sarge, a number of other Phillies-turned-Cubs contributed to the division winning effort. Larry Bowa, Keith Moreland (.279, 16 HR), Bob Dernier (,278, 45 stolen bases), and MVP Ryne Sandberg (.314, 19 HR, 84 RBI, 114 runs scored, 32 steals) were all position players for the '84 Cubs. Ex-Phils Richie Hebner and Jay Johnstone also had some at-bats, while Dick Ruthven, Warren Brusstar, and Dickie Noles all pitched.

As for Sarge, 1984 was his last hurrah. The rigors of the game he played so hard had taken their toll on his 34-year-old body. Matthews played only three more seasons. He never again hit over .260.

Al Holland says, "Sarge was the hardest working outfielder I ever saw. He came to play and he came to win every day. He was an intense competitor. But outside the lines he was like the rest of that '83 team. I never learned so much about the game as I did on that team. I also never had so much fun. And Sarge was in the middle of all the fun. He never stopped needling everybody in the locker room. He was a positive personality to have around the clubhouse."

"Sarge is one of those guys who left a big mark on the organization," Dan Stephenson sums up. "He was unique—a fun guy with a huge personality. He had his own style in everything. Take videos. Some guys study them, some guys ignore them—but either way, they treat them primarily as a learning tool or diagnostic tool. Sarge took a completely different view. To him, they were motivational tools. He used to pop into the video room just to watch himself hit a homer. He'd say something like, 'That was *beautiful!*' Then he'd leave all pumped up."

Below: Avoiding an Eddie Murray tag, Gary Matthews scrambles back to the bag during the 1983 World Series.
Focus on Sport/Getty Images

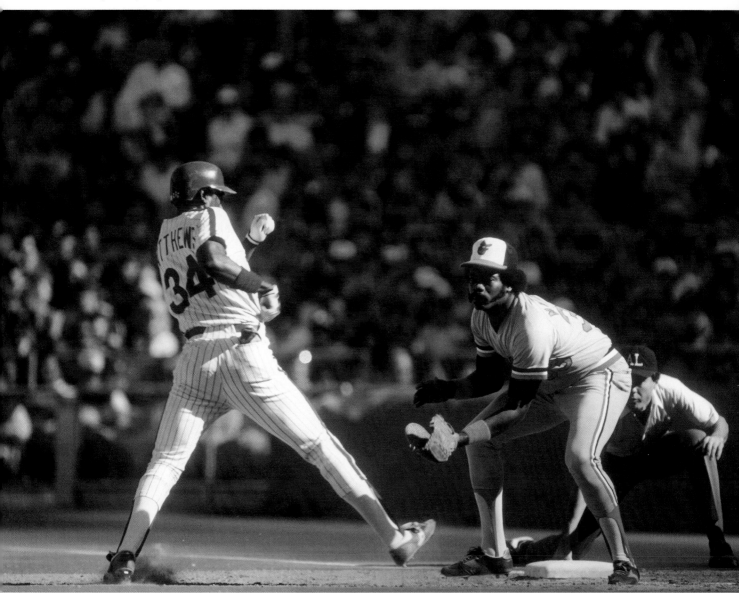

MAJE

Larry Shenk is the Phillies' new kid on the block compared to Maje McDonnell. Fifty-six years ago, a miniscule, skinny pitcher named Robert "Major League" McDonnell from Villanova University pitched an exhibition game against the Phillies. He lost 7-6 but impressed the Phils with his control and poise.

MAJE McDONNELL: "Herb Pennock who used to pitch for the '27 Yankees was the Phils general manager in those days. He liked me cause I threw strikes. Herb wanted me to come on board with the Phils. He told me the Phillies would teach me a new pitch and help me increase my velocity. They did. They tried to show me pitches like the knuckleball. But my hand was too small to grip it. I never mastered any other pitch, and I never gained enough velocity to make the jump to the majors."

Maje actually *did* jump to the majors. He became a Phillies pitcher—but not a member of the pitching staff as he had dreamed. Maje became the batting-practice pitcher. The Phils hired Maje McDonnell the day he graduated from Villanova.

Maje's role for his new employer wasn't limited to pitching batting practice. Teams in that era did-

n't have money for specialists. The '40s and '50s was the era of the jack-of-all-trades. The young ex-Wildcat had his hand in everything. He played pepper with infielders, jogged with the pitchers, shagged flies to the outfielders, and served as all-around gopher.

"I did absolutely anything anybody asked. Anything I figured needed to be done, I took the initiative and did. I did everything Phils manager Ben Chapman needed. Next thing I knew, the Phils promoted me to coach. They gave me the title so I would be eligible for a pension, which was a big issue in baseball at the time. I wouldn't have been eligible for a pension if I were just a batting practice pitcher. The Phils were good to me."

So Maje McDonnell, just three years removed from Villanova University, wound up as the bullpen coach for the pennant-winning 1950 Phillies Whiz Kids. That pennant still ranks as his greatest thrill.

MAJE: "I was young myself that year. I became very close with the guys on that team. That team came so far so fast. Robin Roberts, Curt Simmons, Dick Sisler—we had real gentlemen on that squad. They were great players and polite, humble men. My only regret is that we never beat Brooklyn again. We had too many injuries. We could have competed with Brooklyn or anyone else if we'd have stayed healthy. But too many of our pitchers got hurt, and we just

Left: Maje McDonnell has been a mainstay with the Phillies in several capacities for more than half a century.
Courtesy of the Philadelphia Phillies

couldn't compete. If you check back to that era, you'd find we had Brooklyn's number when we played head to head. Robbie [Robin Roberts] would hook up against Newk [Don Newcombe] in some of the greatest pitching battles I ever saw. Robbie always seemed to come out ahead. Newk was a

"Maje stands for 'Major League,' ever since I can remember, everybody called me 'Major League.' I grew up in the Port Richmond section of Philadelphia and went to St. Anne's Parochial School. I was always running around the neighborhood dribbling a basketball or tossing a baseball. The whole neighborhood started calling me 'Major League.' Then it got shortened to 'Major' and eventually 'Maje.'"

[MAJE McDONNELL—PHILLIES LEGEND]

great pitcher, but we noticed he had a tendency to tire late in the game. When Robbie and Newk locked up, there was a buzz in the dugout all game long, 'Hold on till the later innings, Robbie. We'll get him then.' And Robbie did hold them. Robbie would shut Brooklyn down. Then we'd get to Newk in the eighth or so."

Maje was only one part of an unusual coaching staff in the Whiz Kids era. Eddie Sawyer was the

manager. Like Maje, Sawyer never played or coached major league baseball before he came up to the bigs. Sawyer was out of baseball a few years after his team won the '50 pennant, but Maje stayed on as a Phillie coach till 1957. That netted him the requisite ten years to qualify for a pension.

After '57, Maje scouted and did some other jobs for the Phils. In the '60s, he left the Phillie flock for a few years. Ballantine Beer, one of the Phillies major sponsors in the '50s, wooed him away. Maje served as their goodwill ambassador and worked in the company's marketing/sales division. Maje couldn't keep away from the diamond very long, however. While he was working at Ballantine Beer, he coached baseball at Chestnut Hill Academy. When Bill Giles came to Philadelphia in the late '60s, he looked up Maje and coaxed him back to the Phils. Maje has been there ever since.

Thousands—no, tens of thousands—of fans over the past six decades have grown to love Maje McDonnell. Maje has delivered countless banquet speeches and numerous public appearances in his Phillie career. His shtick could land him on the Borscht Belt circuit. Yet despite his popularity, the average Phillie fan doesn't know where he got the name "Maje."

"Maje stands for 'Major League,'" he winks. "Ever since I can remember, everybody called me 'Major League.' I grew up in the Port Richmond section of Philadelphia and went to St. Anne's Parochial School. I was always running around the neighborhood dribbling a basketball or tossing a baseball. The whole neighborhood started calling me 'Major League.' Then it got shortened to 'Major' and eventually 'Maje.'"

Maje was the first kid from St. Anne's to win a sports scholarship to Villanova. The scholarship was half-baseball/half-basketball. Today's fan would find it hard to believe that a 5-5, 140 pounder could captain the Wildcat basketball team, but Maje McDonnell did. In fact, when he started coaching with the Phillies, Villanova offered him a job as assistant basketball coach. The Phils didn't interfere. They allowed their bullpen coach to pull double duty. During baseball's off season, McDonnell held the post of assistant basketball coach at Villanova. He served in that capacity for over a decade. He had a lot of success on the hardwood too. As far as he (and anyone else) can tell, Maje McDonnell is the only person ever to coach in both a World Series and an NCAA Tournament. Maje simultaneously served as Villanova's freshman basketball coach. One of his teams spun out a perfect 22-0 season. Overall, his freshman teams posted a 117-18 record.

With the Phils, although Maje served primarily as a batting-practice pitcher, he did squeeze in a few mound appearances himself. He pitched for the Phils three times. All three appearances came against minor-league teams in exhibition games. He never gave up a run.

At 80-something, Maje continues to pepper up the Phils offices daily at Citizens Bank Park. He remains a bundle of positive energy and goodwill, same as he ever was.

Above: The day Maje graduated from Villanova in the 1940s, the Phillies hired him to be their batting practice pitcher. Before he knew it, he was a member of the team's coaching staff. *Courtesy of Maje McDonnell*

MAJE: "I've spent so many wonderful years with this organization and this city. I've been very blessed. I've got several World Series rings. I have more wonderful memories than I could ever imagine. I've met the greatest people around these offices. I wouldn't change anything in my life."

TUG McGRAW

"Tug was chaos looking for a place to land." That's the way John McManus describes Tug McGraw. You can usually catch John at Rembrandt's, the bellwether restaurant in Fairmount owned by Jan Zarkin. That's where Tug met John. John became one of Tug's closest friends and a constant companion during the last 15 years of the Tugger's life.

Tug was a great pitcher for the Mets and Phils. In Spring, 2003 he was stricken with brain cancer. On January 5, 2004 Tug succumbed. "I was with him at the end," McManus recalls. "Tug invited a few of his closest friends to Tim's ranch [Tim is country singer Tim McGraw, Tug's son] outside Nashville. Even when Tug was dying, wackiness and chaos surrounded him. We called for a local priest to administer the last rites to him. We waited and waited but he didn't show up. We called the rectory again. They sent a second priest. He did show up and he administered the last rites to Tug. A while later right out of the blue, the 'first' priest shows up at the door. He's all disheveled. It turns out that the guy had gone to the wrong address. Of course he didn't *know* it was the wrong address. The door to this place was open when he arrived, so he went in,

Born: August 30, 1944, Martinez, California
Died: January 5, 2004, Nashville, Tennessee
Position: Relief Pitcher
Years with the Phillies: 1975-1984
Uniform Number: 45
Major League Stats: 96-92, 3.14 ERA, 180 Saves
Postseason Stats: NLCS (1976, 1977, 1978, 1980) and 1981 Divisional Playoff: 1-2, 3.13 ERA; 1980 World Series: 1-1. 1.17 ERA
Honors:
• 1975 Phillie All-Star
• Left-handed Relief Pitcher on 1983 Phils All-Centennial team
• Left-handed Relief Pitcher on the All-Vet team

sat down, and waited for somebody to show up. Somebody showed up, all right. The owners came back, peeked in a window and saw a stranger sitting on their sofa. The owner hustled around to the back of the house, tiptoed inside, sneaked up behind the priest and roughed him up while his wife held a shotgun on him! When the poor priest finally explained why he was there, they let him go and he rode out to Tim's place. Things like that happened to Tug everywhere he went."

Tug died at his son's farm. His body was brought back to the Philly area for private funeral

Left: One of the finest lefthanded relievers in baseball history, Tug McGraw saved 94 games in 10 seasons with the Phillies.
Courtesy of the Philadelphia Phillies

"Aside from being a great pitcher, he had a great sense of humor. I'd walk into the clubhouse and he'd ask, 'LC—you pitching tonight?' When I'd say yes, Tug would shoot back, 'Me too!'"

[LARRY CHRISTENSON—FORMER PHILLIES STARTING PITCHER]

services. Again a priest added a deft twist to the occasion.

"Tug's friend, Father Victor, was giving the eulogy," McManus recounts. "Tim couldn't make it back for the services. So when Father Victor said, 'We're all saddened because a dear member of Tug's family can't join us,' we all thought he was referring to Tim. He wasn't. Father Victor hoisted a bottle of Jamison over his head for the congregation to see. Everyone cracked up, which is just the way Tug would have wanted it!"

Tug was famous/infamous for his love of Jamison's and a number of other adult beverages. He named one of his pitches the "Jamison," because it was "high and tight." Tug came up with lots of zany names for his pitches, like his "Peggy Lee fastball"—so named because batters thought, "Is that all there is?"

"Tug could pitch. He didn't just throw," Larry Christenson says. "Aside from being a great pitcher, he had a great sense of humor. I'd walk into the clubhouse and he'd ask, 'LC—you pitching tonight?' When I'd say yes, Tug would shoot back, 'Me too!'"

Frank Edwin McGraw bounded with energy. He acted that way from birth, literally. His mom is the one who nicknamed him "Tug." Frank Edwin was a breast feeder.

Tug played baseball, football, and basketball in high school. He wasn't a big star.

"His brother Hank was the high school star," McManus contends. The Mets were scouting Hank who said he wouldn't sign unless they gave a tryout to his little brother. That's how Tug got started. The Mets brought Tug down to Florida and he pitched the only no-hitter in his entire life so they kept him around."

Tug came up to the Mets in 1965. Despite an impressive 3.27 ERA, his record was 2-7. One of his staff mates was Warren Spahn, a 4-12 Met pitcher in 1965 closing out a glorious career. McGraw learned the fine points of his craft from listening to Spahn.

"Tug insisted that he never had arm trouble because he modeled his pitching motion after Warren Spahn's," McManus reveals. "Spahn pitched till he was 44 and never had arm trouble. He knew how to use his legs and body in the delivery. His motion saved his arm."

The Mets were awful in 1965. They finished last with a 50-112 record. Within two years, however, Tom Seaver, Nolan Ryan, and Jerry Koosman joined the fold. By 1968, New York had climbed out of the basement for only the second time in history.

Right: Tug McGraw celebrates after recording the final out for the Phillies in their 1980 World Series-clinching Game 6 win over the Kansas City Royals.
Rich Pilling/MLB/Getty Images

Their advance was humble. They moved a single notch up to ninth place. The following season, the Amazin' Mets shocked the world.

Tugger was the emotional kingpin of that '69 crew. He coined the phrase "You Gotta Believe!" which the Mets rode all the way to a world championship. McGraw had the second lowest ERA (2.24) on the staff, right behind Tom Seaver. Tug pitched in with 12 saves, eighth best in the NL. His .750 winning percentage (his record was 9-3) was third best in the NL.

"Tug used to cut the Mets' hair," McManus relates. "That's right. Tug was a barber. The New York union found out he was cutting hair and demanded that he be certified. One day Tug was cutting Yogi Berra's hair. The Mets were on the road at the time. The phone rang and Yogi got on and talked to his wife. Yogi hung up and said his wife must be sick because 'She told me she's going to see *Dr. Zhivago* today.' Tug loved to tell that story!"

"Tug's first manager in the majors was Casey Stengel. Tug liked to tell the story about how Casey comforted him after Tug was tagged with a long-distance homer. Casey sauntered over to Tug on the bench and reassured him, 'Don't feel bad, kid. You must have thrown the ball real hard for him to hit it that far.'"

Tug loved to have fun, but he was a purist about baseball.

"Tug told me he didn't appreciate John Kruk's antics when Randy Johnson almost beaned him in the 1993 All Star game," Tom Burgoyne, the Phillie Phanatic, points out. "Tug was vehement. He insisted that the All-Star game pits the best against the best. Those match-ups were serious business to Tug. It was always surprising to hear Tug talk that way. He was one of the game's greatest clowns, but he was dead serious when the game was going on."

"Tug was dead set against the DH," McManus chimes in. "He *was* a baseball purist. He hated the DH. He used to say the Russians invented it. According to Tug, the Russians couldn't beat us culturally or militarily so they had to subvert our hallowed institutions. The DH was one of their ploys."

That was Tug McGraw—dead serious and competitive. Yet he couldn't resist dressing up everything he did with humor. The trait endeared him to Philadelphians.

"Tug was a broadcaster for awhile," John McManus remembers. "He was notorious for being late. His favorite cover-up and excuse when he walked in late was, 'Sorry, but this is the earliest I've ever been late.' He was always late and he never prepared for anything. We'd be riding down to the TV station so he could tape a segment for the news and all the way down he'd be asking, 'Did the Phils win last night? How have they been doing?' Then the camera would go on and he'd be relaxed and entertaining. Tug was a natural in front of the camera. He was a great adliber. He and Scott Palmer gave a report on the first night game at Wrigley Field. The game was in a rain delay when Tug got on the air. Tug tried to say, 'The *elements* are making it difficult to play tonight.' For some reason—maybe it was Jamison—Tug kept saying, 'The *elephants* are making it difficult to play tonight.' He botched it twice. When he botched it a third time, he just smiled, shrugged, and said, 'Well, there you have it. Couldn't pitch here. Can't talk here!'"

Joe Danko, a bartender at Rembrandt's, recalls a time when Philly's Action News did a segment on Tug, "Tug was in here all excited about going to spring training the next day," Danko says. "Then Action News does this segment about how

Tug was going to Florida to help out with the Phils' young pitching staff. Tug looked at the TV and yelled, 'Like hell. I'm going down to teach them how to pitch with a hangover.'"

Even the stories about Tug's darker side were tinged with slapstick.

"Tug would get ticked sometimes and throw furniture around,' McManus relates. "One day in Pittsburgh, the old Pirate 'Lightning and Lumber Gang' lit him up pretty good. He went back to the hotel and started tossing furniture around the room. He hustled over to the police station and told them, Lon Chaney, Jr.-like, to lock him in a cell for the night so he didn't wreck his room. The cop said they couldn't toss him in jail because they hadn't booked him on anything. So Tug went outside, picked up a rock, and yelled that he was going to toss it at the window unless they locked him up for the night. They accommodated him."

Tug didn't play guitar like his country megastar son, Tim. But he was masterful at striking responsive chords in the hearts of teammates and fans.

"Mike Schmidt took the Tugger's death real hard," John McManus recalls. "Tug and Schmidty used to take turns driving to the Vet. They always stopped on the way to the game and picked up black and white milkshakes. After Tug was hospitalized in Florida, Schmidty visited him every day at the hospital. He never walked into the room without a black and white milkshake."

There are a million Tug McGraw stories. He lived life to the hilt—like the title of his son's latest album, "Live Like You were Dying." Tug didn't go soft into that dark night. He went out the way he came in—tug, tugging into the night.

Right: Tug McGraw took pitching seriously, but enjoyed expressing his unique sense of humor everywhere else.
Brace Photo

DAVE RAYMOND

The Phillie Phanatic is the perennial winner of *USA Today's* annual top professional mascot contest. He (or she or it) remains the uncontested dean of professional sport mascots—the most recognizable mascot in all of professional sport. Over the past 26 years, the Phanatic has waddled, danced, and clowned his way into Philadelphia's collective heart and soul.

Turn on the nightly news in Philly. As the theme music rolls, a collage of local images flit by. The collage gets frequent updates. Old images vanish, replaced by more current ones. But the Phillie Phanatic always lands a slot.

Every summer, the Phanatic's mug adorns Free Library posters that exhort kids to read. You see them all over the city. The Phanatic pops up frequently in commercials, boorishly bursts on to Philly TV sets, and guest stars at City galas and happenings.

The Phanatic makes about 500 local appearances a year. However, his celebrity extends well beyond his own 'hood. He also logs numerous trips nationwide to minor-league cities whose teams have no affiliation with the Phillies. He's there simply because baseball fans, whether they're Phillie fans or not, get a kick out of watching him.

Left: Dave Raymond rests alongside the costume that made him a Philadelphia institution. Raymond donned the Phanatic costume for Phillies home games, and countless other events, from 1978 through 1993.
Courtesy of Dave Raymond

Major League Baseball also taps the Phanatic as an ambassador. He has accompanied the Major League all-star team on three tours of Japan. Philly's mascot has rolled out his act on five different continents as a representative of MLB.

Bill Giles of the Phillies came up with the mascot idea in the mid-'70s. As Giles recalls, "I had no idea what a mascot would actually *do* when we first kicked the idea around. But I was convinced that the right guy could really run with it."

Selling the Phils' organization on a mascot wasn't easy. When the Phils' brass grilled Giles at a meeting about the specifics of his mascot proposal, their first question was, "Who will be the mascot? Who's the guy inside the suit?" Bill unabashedly confesses he wasn't prepared. Bill doesn't sweat the small stuff. In response, Giles tossed out the name "Dave Raymond."

Who is Dave Raymond? Well at the time, he wasn't even a Phillies employee. Dave was a full-time student at the University of Delaware finishing up his undergraduate degree. The previous summer he had worked as a Phillies intern. His outgoing personality and self-assuredness—well okay, Giles called it cockiness—impressed Giles. Bill believed Raymond could pack proper persona into the costume.

So the Phillies pitched the job to Dave Raymond. They extended him practically a carte blanche to develop "the mascot job."

"When the Phils called, I was set to graduate from college," Dave says. "I was about to get my degree and the Phils wanted me to slip into a mascot suit and do 'whatever.' I was scared to even bring it up with my parents. I could just imagine their reaction."

Their reaction surprised him. Dave's parents endorsed the idea. His dad is Tubby Raymond. At the time, Tubby was Delaware's football coach—a local legend on the road to notching 300 career victories. Dave was the Blue Hens' punter (Dave's exploits at Delaware require a separate book). His

In accepting the "job," Dave's challenge was to animate a lifeless mascot, to give it personality and soul—to play the monster to Bill Giles's Dr. Frankenstein.

"The Phillies gave me plenty of leeway—artistic freedom, you might say," Dave elaborates. "Basically, I tried to create a personality I thought everyone could relate to. The Phanatic became the guy who 'gets away' with the things the average guy can't, but wishes he could. The Phanatic gets away with goosing the umpire. He gets away with buffing the baldheaded guy minding his own business innocently watching the game. The Phanatic gets away with standing on top of the dugout or dancing with pretty girls in the stadium, and hugging and kissing them. I'm making it sound like too much fun, aren't I?"

Looks are deceiving. Being the Phillie Phanatic can be a tough job—or at

> ## "My parents loved the Phillies organization. They also believed you have to take advantage of opportunities that pop up in life. In their opinion, the Phillie Phanatic job was an opportunity that could lead anywhere. They advised me to go for it. I'm glad I listened."
>
> [DAVE RAYMOND—ORIGINAL PHILLIE PHANATIC]

parents encouraged him to get an education and a substantial job. However they were convinced that a career in the field of sports, in any capacity, presented a promising career path.

DAVE RAYMOND: "My parents loved the Phillies organization. They also believed you have to take advantage of opportunities that pop up in life. In their opinion, the Phillie Phanatic job was an opportunity that could lead anywhere. They advised me to go for it. I'm glad I listened."

least a demanding one. At times it can be exhausting. On a torrid Philadelphia July Sunday, walking across Death Valley might seem like an arctic vacation to the guy trapped inside the Phanatic costume. Kids maul and paw the Phanatic incessantly. But Dave Raymond thrived in that scenario. He's hard wired that way. He's a born entertainer with a great sense of humor and a gift for mime.

DAVE RAYMOND: "My mother was deaf so I learned to sign. Because of signing, pantomime came about naturally. I discovered I could act out what people were feeling and when I did, the fans responded tremendously. Philly people ate up the whole Phanatic act from day one."

Day One was April 25, 1978. The Phanatic donned his costume and headed into the Phillie throng with no plan other than "to make something happen." Which he did. Dave walked into the seating sections at the Vet and created mayhem. In no time at all, the Phillie Phanatic was embraced as an integral part of the Veterans Stadium scene.

Dave Raymond has moved on. Following the 1993 season, he turned the Phanatic costume over to Tom Burgoyne. Dave now runs his own business in Delaware. He creates new mascots and characters. He also consults on mascot-related projects with professional sport franchises and other businesses countrywide.

Tom Burgoyne remains the Phillie Phanatic. Tom has to be accorded equal recognition for the ubiquitous mascot's continued success. Tom's challenge was arguably equal to that of his predecessor. Many Philadelphia fans thought the Phillie Phanatic would die when Dave Raymond departed. The opposite occurred. The Phanatic's cachet has grown. Twenty-seven years since the Phanatic first waddled onto the Philly scene, the Phillie Phanatic is as much a part of the old ballgame in Phillytown as peanuts and Cracker Jacks—and Schmitters and cheesesteaks too.

Below: The Phillie Phanatic looks down from its perch atop Veterans Stadium in April 1991. The Phanatic was camping out on the roof awaiting the team's home opener. *AP/WWP*

ROBIN ROBERTS

Robin Roberts, along with Richie Ashburn, remains the most enduring name from the Whiz Kids. Robin Roberts dominated the NL pitching ranks in the early '50s. From 1950 through 1955, Robbie won 138 games, more than any other major league pitcher in the first half of the decade. Fellow Hall of Famer Warren Spahn places second on that list. He trails Robbie by a whopping 20 wins. That's an average of three wins a year. The ninth guy on the list happens to be Roberts's stablemate Curt Simmons. Curt's 69 victories amounts to *one-half* of Robbie's total. That means that only eight pitchers in all of baseball topped *half* of Roberts's wins.

Comparing that six-year slice at the acme of Roberts's career with similar slices from a couple of other dominant pitchers—Sandy Koufax and Steve Carlton—intimates how dominant Roberts was in his prime.

Koufax enjoyed his greatest years from 1961 through 1966. His 129 wins in that stretch topped all his peers. Koufax however won nine fewer games than Robbie did in his six best years. The Dodger great also had the benefit of a 162-game season in all but one of those years.

Left: The most dominant pitcher of his time, Robin Roberts started five of the six All-Star games from 1950-1955.
Photo File/MLB/Getty Images

Born: September 30, 1926, Springfield, Illinois
Position: Pitcher
Years with the Phillies: 1948-1961
Uniform Number: 36
Major League Stats: 286-246, 3.41 ERA, 25 Saves
Phillies Postseason Stats: 1950 World Series: 0-1, 2.27 ERA
Honors:
• Selected to seven consecutive All-Star games from 1950-1956 and started all but two of them ('52 and '56)
• Shares the record for most All-Star starts with Lefty Grove and Don Drysdale
• Named Player of the Year by *The Sporting News* in 1952
• Chosen three times as *The Sporting News's* Pitcher of the Year before the Cy Young Award was established
• Uniform number 36 was retired by the Phillies in 1962
• Elected to the Hall of Fame in 1976
• In 1978, first Phillie inducted into the Philadelphia Wall of Fame
• In 1983, chosen as starting right-handed pitcher for the Phillies' All-Centennial team.

Koufax edged out the runnerup on his list, Juan Marichal, by only five wins—far short of the 20-win edge that Roberts held over Spahn. And you need to drop down 14 slots on the Koufax list—as compared to only eight on the Roberts's list—before you reach a guy with one-half of Sandy's wins. Who was the pitcher with half of Sandy's wins from '61-'66? Ironically, it was the same guy on Roberts's list—Curt Simmons.

As for Carlton, his most productive six-year consecutive stint fell between 1971 and 1976. Carlton was a St. Louis Cardinal in 1971 when he first reached the 20-win plateau. He followed up with his most remarkable season. He tallied 27 wins as a Phillie in 1972. His wins accounted for 46

that name again) was tapped for the honor. No pitcher *has ever done that*. Despite those impressive statistics, it took a few years for Robin Roberts to get inducted into the Hall of Fame.

BOBBY SHANTZ: "It's hard to believe it took Robbie so long to get into the Hall of Fame. I think he and Bob Lemon were the greatest pitchers of my era, along with Warren Spahn. It's hard to pick the greatest because guys like Allie Reynolds got hurt when they were young and never had the chance to put up big career numbers. Early Wynn, Sal Maglie, Don Newcombe, Vic Raschi, Eddie Lopat—they were a few of the great pitchers from that era. But Spahn, Lemon, and Robbie, I think,

"I was fortunate as a pitcher. I had terrific defensive players behind me. Eddie Waitkus was as smooth as they come at first base. Granny could play any position in the infield and do the job."

[ROBIN ROBERTS—HALL OF FAME PITCHER]

percent of his club's total. Over Carlton's best six-year stretch, he won 111 games, 27 short of Roberts's total. Hall of Famers Don Sutton (110) and Tom Seaver (107) were close runners-up in total wins. And you have to drop all the way down to slot No. 29 before you reach the pitcher whose victories total half of Carlton's (No it's not Simmons this time. It's Don Wilson).

Roberts started *every* All-Star Game for the National League from 1950 through 1955, except for 1952 when teammate Curt Simmons (there's

were the greatest. They all deserved to go right into the Hall of Fame."

Robin Roberts was one of the first "bonus babies" of the Bob Carpenter era. When Carpenter took over in 1943, the Phils were a rudderless franchise. They had finished in last place the previous

Right: Robin Roberts defined the term workhorse, pitching at least 300 innings every season from 1950 through 1955.
Courtesy of the Philadelphia Athletics Historical Society

"The Hall of Fame was a great honor. I met lots of wonderful people in baseball. My strongest associations, I think, will always be with the Whiz Kids. . . . I remained close friends all my life with those guys. It was such a wonderful experience going through that 1950 pennant race and coming out on top. But yes, the Hall of Fame induction was terrific."

[ROBIN ROBERTS—HALL OF FAME PITCHER]

five consecutive years. It had been more than a decade since they finished higher than next to last. Carpenter set about building a solid organization, top to bottom. Offering young players serious bonus money to sign was a cornerstone of his organizational philosophy.

"People ask me why I signed with the Phillies," Robin Roberts reflects. "It's simple. They offered me the most money. I was raised in Springfield, Illinois, so I didn't grow up being a Phillies fan. I always wanted to play a sport professionally. I was playing basketball for Michigan State University at the time, but when I was offered $25,000 to play baseball—and that was a lot of money in those days—I accepted. All I was looking for was enough money to buy a new home for my parents. That was enough in those days. Looking back, I could have gotten more if I knew then what I know now."

Robbie started his career as a power pitcher. He was known for his "nice guy" approach to the art of pitching. In an era when it was commonplace for pitchers to dust off batters (Robbie's con-

temporary Sal Maglie was nicknamed "The Barber" because of the "close shaves" he gave hitters), Robbie refused to dust anyone off. His strength was pinpoint control. He coupled a fastball that moved with dogged determination to achieve greatness. He was an inveterate workhorse. He led the NL in victories from 1952 through 1955 (chalking up 28, 23, 23, and 23 wins successively). However he also led the *majors* in innings pitched every year from 1951 through 1955. He hurled more than 300 innings every year from 1950 through 1955. As a frame of reference, Steve Carlton in 1980 was the last major leaguer to pitch 300 innings in a season.

The first year Robbie failed to pitch 300 innings was 1956. He pitched *only* 297-1/3 innings. It was also the first time in seven seasons he didn't win 20. He won 19.

The wear and tear took its toll. When Robbie lost a few inches off his fastball, he seemed to be washed up. After 19 wins in 1956, his record sank to 10-22 for the 77-77 Phils in 1957.

He wasn't through, though. Robbie reinvented himself as a finesse pitcher in 1958. He bettered his record to 17-14 and won the Associated Press Comeback Player of the Year Award. At that point, however, the aging legend no longer figured in the Phillies' plans. New names like Chico Fernandez, Ed Bouchee, Harry the Horse Anderson, Jack Sanford, Bob Bowman, and Pancho Herrera were replacing the old guard. By 1960, the cast of the Whiz Kids was gone. Granny Hamner, Del Ennis, Stan Lopata, Andy Seminick, and Richie Ashburn had all been traded. Only Roberts and Simmons remained. When Simmons was dealt to St. Louis in 1961, Roberts became the Whiz Kids' sole survivor.

Robbie went a miserable 1-10 that season and was traded to Baltimore. Over the next three campaigns as an Oriole, he twirled a 37-29 record, sporting a winning record all three years.

His accomplishments eventually landed him in Cooperstown. He was inducted in 1976 on his third try.

ROBIN ROBERTS: "The Hall of Fame was a great honor. I met lots of wonderful people in baseball. My strongest associations, I think, will always be with the Whiz Kids. Granny Hamner, Del Ennis, Puddinhead Jones, Andy Seminick, Richie Ashburn—so many great guys and great ballplayers. I remained close friends all my life with those guys. It was such a wonderful experience going through that 1950 pennant race and coming out on top. But yes, the Hall of Fame induction was terrific. I was delighted when Richie finally got the recognition he deserves too."

Today Robbie lives in Florida. He has written a few books with co-author Paul Rogers. And you can still catch Robbie at numerous sport memorabilia shows around the country.

PHILLIES' PITCHERS WHO HAVE STARTED AN ALL-STAR GAME

1950	Robin Roberts (1)
1951	Robin Roberts (2)
1952	Curt Simmons
1953	Robin Roberts (3)
1954	Robin Roberts (4)
1955	Robin Roberts (5)
1979	Steve Carlton
1993	Terry Mulholland
1999	Curt Schilling

MOST WINS, SINGLE SEASON, PHILADELPHIA PHILLIES

38	1890	Kid Gleason
33	1916	Grover Cleveland Alexander
32	1880	Lee Richmond
32	1892	Gus Wehing
31	1915	Grover Cleveland Alexander
30	1886	Charlie Ferguson
30	1917	Grover Cleveland Alexander
28	1889	Charlie Buffington
28	1890	Charlie Buffington
28	1887	Dan Casey
28	1911	Grover Cleveland Alexander
28	1952	Robin Roberts

MIKE SCHMIDT

Mike Schmidt's 1973 rookie season gave little indication he was marching toward Cooperstown. Schmidt hit for a lower rookie average—.196—than any other Hall of Famer. Yet in the ensuing 16 years, he elevated his performance to such heights that *Total Baseball*, the game's "bible," ranks Mike Schmidt as the 12th best ballplayer of all time. That flip-flop—from batting below the Mendoza Line to inclusion in baseball's diamond dozen—make Rocky Balboa's final-round comebacks in the ring seem plausible.

Despite his anemic batting average as a rookie, Schmidt flashed long-distance pop. He slammed 18 homers in 367 plate appearances. He provided his definition of "power hitter" to the local press early in his career. Schmidt opined that a power hitter was a guy who didn't need to get all of a pitch to knock it out of the yard. Mike Schmidt fit that definition.

He didn't need to get all of the ball to go yard. When he did get a hold of one, he hit some prodigious shots. One of his more memorable blasts was launched in the old Astrodome. It

Left: Mike Schmidt, considered by many to be the greatest third baseman of all time, knocked out 548 home runs during his 18-year career.
Courtesy of the Philadelphia Phillies

Born: September 27, 1949, Dayton, Ohio
Position: First Base, Third Base
Years with the Phillies: 1972-1989
Uniform Number: 20
Major League Stats: .267, 548 HR, 1,595 RBI
Phillies Postseason Stats: NLCS ('76, '77, '78, '80, '83) and '81 Division Playoff: .242, 2 HR, 9 RBI; '80 World Series: .381, 2 HR, 7 RBI; '83 World Series: .050, 0 HR, 0 RBI
Honors:
- Inducted into Hall of Fame 1995
- NL MVP, 1980, 1981, 1986
- TSN NL Player of the Year, 1980, 1986
- World Series MVP, 1980
- Silver Slugger Award, 1980, 1981, 1982, 1983, 1984, 1986
- Rawlings Gold Glove Award, 1976, 1977, 1978, 1979, 1980, 1981, 1982, 1983, 1984, 1986
- NL Player of the Week, 1976, 1980, 1984, 1986
- NL Player of the Month, April 1976, July 1979, May 1980, August 1981, July 1982
- Inducted into Philadelphia Phillies Wall of Fame 1990
- Chosen for Phillies Centennial Team
- Chosen for Phillies All-Vet team
- Named Baseball Player of the Decade (1980s) by *The Sporting News*
- Voted Greatest Phillie Player Ever by 1983 fan poll
- Picked as third baseman on MasterCard's All Century Team.

slammed into a ceiling-mounted speaker and bounced back down on to the field of play … for a long single. Onlookers were flabbergasted that anyone could hit one that high and far.

"Schmidty was the greatest athlete the Phillies ever had," teammate Larry Christenson contends. "He could play any sport. He could run and throw. He had incredible hand-eye coordination. He could have been an NFL quarterback if it weren't for his bad knees. Honestly, I think deep down that's exactly what he would like to have been—a quarterback. He wanted to join the pro golf circuit after his baseball career too. That's why he admired John Elway and John Brodie so

hearts of the Philly fans despite a list of accomplishments that could fill dozens of pages.

"To outsiders, I think Mike was an enigma," Phillies VP of PR Larry Shenk explains. "If you contrast him with Pete Rose and Steve Carlton, you get an idea of why that was. Pete was Mr. Media. He was always willing and eager to appear in front of the public. Pete thought that was simply good business. It increased his earning power. Steve Carlton refused to talk to the press. He established that policy in his second season and never deviated from it, so Lefty was predictable. Mike fell somewhere in between. Sometimes he liked doing interviews. Other times he avoided

"Schmidty was the greatest athlete the Phillies ever had. He could play any sport. He could run and throw. He had incredible hand-eye coordination. He could have been an NFL quarterback if it weren't for his bad knees."

[LARRY CHRISTENSON—FORMER PHILLIES PITCHER]

much. They were both quarterbacks *and* golfers. Schmidty never got quite good enough to compete on the pro circuit, but he is a great golfer, too."

The cat-quick Schmidt was a great enough fielder to earn ten Gold Gloves at third base. He retired as the No. 7 home run hitter of all time. He possessed good speed. His 174 career stolen bases place him eighth on the Phils' all-time list. He slugged more than twice as many career homers as any other Phillie in history. He was selected as the greatest Phillie of all time by a fan vote in 1983. Nevertheless, Schmidt never really won the

them. People read different things into his inconsistency. The thing is, though, most players are that way. It just isn't noticeable. It was with Mike Schmdit because he was such a big star. Everyone was seeking him out every day.

"I'll tell you a funny story about Mike. After we won the final game of the '80 Series, I asked Chris Wheeler to bring Schmidty out to the interview room. Wheels wasn't in the booth at that point. He was my assistant. Schmidty accom-

Right: Mike Schmidt poses in the dugout during the 1980 season. With 48 home runs, Schmidt led the major leagues in round-trippers and led the Phillies to a world championship.
Focus on Sports/Getty Images

modated us, but he wound up in the interview room for such a long time that he missed the postgame show in the Phillies clubhouse. Rose, Dallas Green—everyone had been interviewed on national TV during the clubhouse celebration. Schmidty missed it all. He never forgot it either. He rides me about it to this day. He tells me, 'I'm the only World Series MVP in history who didn't get interviewed in the clubhouse after the win!'

"We had fun with Schmidty at the closing ceremonies at the Vet. I came up with the idea for a Final Innings ceremony where Carlton, Schmidt, and Tug McGraw would each come out separately and reenact one of their great moments. We were concerned about Tug. Physically he was failing badly. Tug was the one who wasn't worried, though. Schmidty and Lefty were! Lefty kept telling me his arm was sore and he couldn't throw. Schmidty said he had a sprained wrist and didn't think he could swing a bat. When the time came though, they all loved it. They all shined. Those guys simply have a lot of pride. They don't ever want to look bad out there. We finished Schmidt's segment off by having Jim Thome run out on the field to greet him after he circled the bases. It was kind of like passing of the baton. Schmidt improvised when he lifted Thome's arm up in the air. It was a great touch."

Jim Thome agrees, "Philly fans might not be aware that I came up as a third baseman. When I was a kid, even though I was a Cubs fan, I idolized Schmidty because he was a power hitter like I hoped to be. Schmidty was the ballplayer I dreamed of becoming. He was also the best fielding third baseman in baseball."

"Mike was amazing with the glove, the greatest third baseman ever," Christenson continues. "Sure he had his little funks out there occasionally. He called them his 'tricky wickets.' But generally, he was incredible. The trouble was, he made everything look so easy. The fans thought he was lackadaisical. Phillie fans don't like lackadaisical. They like guys who look and act intense. That wasn't Mike. He was the definition of cool in everything he did. He was the fashion leader on the team. He dressed cool. He had that curly hair for a long while when it was the height of style. But the fact is: *no one* was more intense about his game. Fans could never imagine how much it bothered Mike when he wasn't playing up to the standards he set for himself."

Al Holland adds, "Schmidty set higher standards for himself than anyone else could possibly set for him. When he didn't come through like he thought he should, it destroyed him inside. He never stopped working to fine tune his skills."

"Yeah," Larry Christenson wraps up, "Schmidty would analyze and analyze. I can still see him holding court at his locker, philosophizing about hitting. Everyone would be listening real intently. Then the Bull [Greg Luzinski] would walk by wearing a towel. He'd interrupt [you might say he butted in], and yell, 'Yo Schmidty. Forget all that. It's simple. See ball. Hit ball. That's all you have to do.'"

Right: Mike Schmidt's able handling of the hot corner earned him 10 Gold Gloves. In fact, he made difficult plays look so easy that some Philly fans called him "lackadaisical".
VJ Lovero/Icon SMI

BOBBY SHANTZ

Bobby Shantz had a short Philadelphia Phillies career. He spent only a portion of one year in Phillie pinstripes. The year, however, happened to be 1964, the most cursed and traumatic year in Philly sport history.

Philadelphia has emerged as one of the country's top 10 tourist destination cities due primarily to its rich history. Still most Philadelphians are unaware of much of the city's history. They couldn't tell you anything about the five apocalyptic yellow fever epidemics that struck Philly in its colonial era. Most modern residents don't know that influenza claimed 13,000 Philadelphia lives in 1918. Traumas like that have drifted into pop oblivion. But *every* sport fan in Philly knows about 1964 whether they were alive at the time or not. Philly fans still *feel* 1964. Presumably in 2064, Philly fans will still reel from the trauma of 1964. The Phils blew a six and a half-game lead with 12 games left to play in that accursed season. Unfortunately, although Bobby Shantz' stint as a Phil was short, he managed to play a role in that debacle.

Shantzy came to the '64 Phils in midseason by way of the Cubs. He pitched only 32 innings for the Phils, all in relief. His numbers were

Born: September 26, 1925, Pottstown, Penn.
Position: Pitcher
Year with the Phillies: 1964
Uniform Number
Major League Stats: 119-99, 3.38 ERA, 48 Saves
Honors:
• 1952 AL MVP

impressive. His record stood at 1-1 and his ERA was a sparkling 2.25. Shantz' most memorable appearance as a Phil, however, overshadowed the good stuff.

On September 26, the Phils were trying desperately to halt a five-game losing skid. Phil hurler Art Mahaffey was on the hill. The Phils were leading when Bobby entered the fray in relief.

"Rico Carty hit a triple off me. That did it. The Braves beat us," Bobby quips. "I think that was the only run I gave up the whole time I was in Philly! Not really, but I did pitch pretty well that season. The problem is—no one remembers. The only thing anyone remembers is that triple! I always joked with [centerfielder] Tony Gonzalez that he could have caught the ball. He was playing too shallow. Tony always says the same thing, 'If I was any deeper I would have been sitting in the stands!'"

Left: A midseason acquisition during the infamous 1964 season, Philadelphia fans remember Bobby Shantz more for the triple he gave up to Rico Carty than his 1-1 record and 2.25 ERA.
Courtesy of the Philadelphia Phillies

"I did pitch pretty well [in 1964]. The problem is—no one remembers. The only thing anyone remembers is that triple!"

[BOBBY SHANTZ—FORMER PHILLIES RELIEVER]

The day after Carty's triple won the game, Johnny Callison hammered three homers and the Phils still came up short—way short. They dropped their seventh straight contest 12-7. They continued the nightmare by losing three more games the next three days.

As for Bobby Shantz, he called it quits after 1964.

"I didn't retire because of that '64 season," Shantzy jokes. "I had a long career. I had been pitching in pain for years. I was ready to call it quits at that point."

He went out like a champ—on a 3.16 ERA in his final season (that ERA includes his stints with the Cubs and Cards). Arguably, Bobby Shantz would have been a Hall of Fame candidate had he not lost so much time to injuries and pain. Despite constant physical problems, Shantz went 119-99 for his career, with a 3.38 ERA in 1,935 1/3 innings pitched.

Shantzy was a Philly local. He grew up in Pottstown and graduated from Pottstown High School. Everyone always considered him too small to play professionally.

BOBBY SHANTZ: "I was only 4-11 in high school. I never pitched. I played outfield. I started pitching when I was in the service. I had trouble getting into the service because of my height. They rejected me the first time I tried to enlist. I came back an inch taller a year later and they accepted me.

"While I was in the service, I played a lot of baseball. I also grew six inches and gained about 50 pounds."

That growth spurt rocketed Bobby Shantz all the way up to 5-6, 139 pounds, hardly the kind of physique that makes pro scouts salivate. Bobby Shantz returned from the war and started working at the Disston Saw Mill in Philly's Tacony section. He also played baseball and football with some local sandlot teams like Forest Hill. While he was pitching for the semi-pro Souderton His Nibs (that's not a misprint and Bobby Shantz has no idea where the name came from), he drew the attention of Harry O'Donnell, a scout for the Philadelphia A's.

BOBBY SHANTZ: "Jocko Collins, who scouted for the Phillies, told me I was too small. Years later, he told me he thought he made a mistake. I told him he didn't. I thought I was too small, too."

Shantz turned out to be one of Philadelphia's many mound giants. He achieved what only one other Philadelphia pitcher—Lefty Grove—had ever done. Shantz won the American League MVP. The year was 1952, an unforgettable year for Shantz and Philadelphia pitchers in general. Though Shantz went 24-7, his win total did not lead the majors. It didn't even lead in *Philadelphia*. The Phils' Robin Roberts won 28 and sported a gaudy 28-7 record.

At the All-Star break, Curt Simmons, the other half of the Phils' one-two pitching punch, was chosen to start the All-Star game. The game was played in Philly at Shibe Park (which was to be renamed Connie Mack Stadium one year later). Philadelphia clamored for an all-Philly mound match-up—Simmons versus Shantz. However, Vic Raschi was given the honor for the Americans. When Shantz made his appearance in the bottom of the fifth, he put on the greatest mid-summer classic pitching exhibition since Carl Hubbell's in 1934. Hubbell had fanned five straight future Hall of Famers: Babe Ruth, Lou Gehrig, Jimmie Foxx, Al Simmons, and Joe Cronin (in the 1984 All-Star game on the 50th anniversary of Hubbell's All-Star feat, Fernando Valenzuela and Dwight Gooden combined to break King Carl's mark by fanning six in a row. Hubbell incidentally threw out the game's first ball). Shantz faced and stuck out three National Leaguers before the skies opened and halted the exhibition. Two of the three—Jackie Robinson and Stan Musial—became Hall of Famers. The other, Whitey Lockman, was a solid star of the early '50s who finished among the top ten NL batsmen that year.

Unfortunately, that glorious 1952 season ended tragically for Shantz.

BOBBY SHANTZ: "Mr. Mack (A's manager Connie Mack) always told me I should bat left-handed to protect my pitching arm. See that way, my left arm wouldn't be exposed to the pitch. But I batted rightie my whole life. I tried but I couldn't switch. I should have tried harder. Towards the end of '52, I had to duck away from a pitch that was coming right at me. Walt Masterson threw it. Walt was another guy who was born in Philadelphia. When I threw up my arm to protect myself, the ball hit my hand and broke it."

Because of the injury, Shantz slumped to 5-9 the next season. He moved out with the A's when the franchise left Philly for Kansas City in 1954, but due to injury hurled only eight innings that season. In 1956, he managed only a 2-7 log with the 52-102 Kansas City Athletics. Salvation was at hand. In 1957, like countless A's of the era, Shantz shipped out to New York. There, like so many others, he found new life.

BOBBY SHANTZ: "Casey [Stengel, the Yankees legendary manager] had me slotted for the bullpen. Then Whitey Ford got hurt and he moved me up to starter. I was 9-1 at the All-Star break and was picked for the All-Star game. When Whitey came back, I went back to the 'pen and never started again."

Bobby starred in the bullpen for the Yanks through 1960. He was on the mound when Tony Kubek got whomped in the Adam's apple on a bad hop, apparent double-play grounder. Up till that point, Shantz had just pitched three strong innings and appeared to be cruising along, preserving a 7-4 Yankee lead.

After the Kubek grounder, Casey Stengel yanked Bobby and ushered in Jim Coates, setting the stage for Ralph Terry, another ex-Athletic. Terry served up Bill Mazeroski's walk-off, Series-winning homer. Philadelphians are painfully aware that there only is one other Series-winning, walk-off homer in history. That's the one Joe Carter hit in '93 off the Phils' Mitch Williams.

The following season, Bobby donned the uniform of the '60 World Series champions. "The Pirates rode me pretty good about that," Bobby jokes. Shantz remained in the National League till 1964. Eventually his career came full circle. He finished in his hometown, playing for Philly's *other* team, which had become Philly's only team.

Richie Ashburn always insisted that Bobby Shantz was the greatest fielding pitcher in history. Shantz won eight straight Gold Glove Awards. He would have won a lot more, but the Gold Glove wasn't instituted till 1957—the latter half of his career. Nevertheless, he remains one of only two pitchers to win the Gold Glove in both leagues. Ex-Phil Jim Kaat is the other. Shantz won four Gold Gloves in the NL and four in the AL. Only Jim Kaat (16) and Greg Maddux (14 and counting) have won more.

After his retirement from baseball, Bobby Shantz owned and operated the Pit-Catch bowling alley and restaurant in Chalfont. He has long since retired from that business. Nowadays, Bobby can be found daily—no matter what the temperature is—shooting in the low 70s on Curt Simmons's Limekiln Golf Course.

JIM THOME

The Phils have fielded some fine first sackers in their 122-year history. The list includes Ed Delahanty, Fred Luderus, Dolph Camilli, Don Hurst, Dick Sisler, Eddie Waitkus, Bill White, Deron Johnson, Dick Allen, Pete Rose, John Kruk, and Rico Brogna. Mike Schmidt even manned first for a while. Jim Thome is the latest one to carry on the tradition. If Thome even approaches what he did in Cleveland, he just might rewrite the all-time Phillies record book for first sackers. He certainly rewrote Cleveland's book.

In 12 years with the Tribe, Thome set the Cleveland standard for most home runs in a single season (52 in 2002) and most home runs in a career (Thome hit 334. Albert Belle is a distant second with 242). Thome also occupies the second position on Cleveland's all-time RBI list. The 927 runners he plated sandwich him between two Hall of Famers on the Cleveland list—Earl Averil, and Nap Lajoie (who played part of his career for the Phillies).

Thome holds the Cleveland record for most consecutive games with a homer (seven), most consecutive seasons with 20 or more homers

Born: August 27, 1970, Peoria, Illinois
Position: First Base
Years with the Phillies: 2003-Current
Uniform Number: 25
Major League Stats (Through 2004): .284, 423 HR, 1,163 RBIs
Honors:
• 2002 recipient of the John Hancock Roberto Clemente Award presented annually to the major league player who exemplifies Clemente's passion for the game, sportsmanship, and community involvement
• Named the Marvin Miller Man of the Year in 2001 for his community involvement
• Served as honorary co-chairman of the United Way Home Run Derby 1998-2002
• 2003 Pro Athlete of the Year by the Philadelphia Sportswriters Association
• NL Player of the Week August 11-17, 2003
• NL Player of the Month September 2003.

(nine), and most consecutive seasons with thirty or more homers (seven). In fact, at this point he is in hot pursuit of the immortal Jimmy Foxx's *former* record of 12 consecutive seasons with 30-plus homers. In 2004, Barry Bonds upped the mark to 13 straight seasons—and

Left: In his first two seasons in Philadelphia, Jim Thome totaled 89 home runs and 236 RBIs.
Courtesy of the Philadelphia Phillies

counting. As of 2004, Thome's string stands at nine—and counting. Big Jim also shares the major league record for most home runs in a Division Series (eight).

Thome arrived in Philly as a ballyhooed free agent in 2003. He left Cleveland—a fervent baseball town—with regret. He had a fine career there, and a fine relationship with the fans.

"I'll never forget his press conference when he announced he was coming to Philly," Dan Stephenson of the Phils video department recalls. "You could tell he was a sincere, good guy. Someone asked him how his wife felt about moving to Philly. Jim's wife is a Cleveland native. Jim replied that he would never have come to Philly

over the Philly fans. The process started before he ever suited up in Phillie pinstripes.

"When we gave Jim a tour of the city—Bill Giles and a lot of the Phillies' brass were in the entourage—we rode by the new park (Citizens Bank Park was under construction when Thome first arrived)," Ruben Amaro, Phils' Assistant General Manager, former batboy, and former outfielder recounts. "Construction on the new ballpark was proceeding at full throttle.

"Construction workers at the new park started hooting and hollering for Thome when they saw the entourage go by. The guys from Electrical Union Local 98 had made special red hats with 'Philadelphia Wants Jim Thome' writ-

"I'm really a blue-collar kind of a guy. I like to come to the park every day and work hard. I always heard that Phillies' fans respected that kind of attitude. When I met the union guys, it I convinced me that Philly was the right fit for me."

[JIM THOME—PHILLIES FIRST BASEMAN]

unless his wife supported the decision. He paused and said, 'My wife's my rock.' Then he got so emotional he had to leave. He came back eight minutes later and told everyone, 'I apologize for leaving like that. I hate when my allergies kick up.' Then he resumed the conference."

Jim is a throwback ballplayer—the increasingly rare performer who feels he owes something to the fans. Thome's sincerity and work ethic won

ten on them. Thome insisted on pulling over and talking with them. You could tell he felt at home with these guys. They all bonded right away."

Jim Thome adds, "I'm really a blue-collar kind of a guy. I like to come to the park every day and work hard. I always heard that Phillies' fans respected that kind of attitude. When I met the

Right: After a tearful farewell to fans in Cleveland, where he spent his first 12 seasons, Jim Thome was all smiles when he arrived in Clearwater, Florida, for his first spring training with the Phillies.
Robert Seale/TSN/Icon SMI

union guys, it I convinced me that Philly was the right fit for me. Plus, I saw that beautiful new ballpark going up. You could see even then it was going to be special. I thought the new park would be a terrific place for Andrea [Jim's wife] and Lila Grace [their daughter] to grow up watching baseball."

Jim Thome grew up watching and playing baseball. He was raised near Peoria, Illinois, in a baseball family that rooted for the Cubs. Thome saw major league baseball live for the first time at Wrigley Field.

"When I went to Wrigley Field, I jumped onto the field to get an autograph from some of the Cubs players," Jim chuckles. "I guess I got a little carried away. But I knew even then that I wanted to play this game for a living. I think baseball is just in my blood."

At Limestone High School in Illinois, Jim Thome earned All-State honors in both baseball and basketball.

"I knew early on that baseball was my game," Jim reflects. "I wasn't going to make it in hoops. When Cleveland selected me in the June '89 draft, I was thrilled. I reported to the Gulf Coast Indians right afterward. I did pretty well in the minors. I

was serious about playing professional ball and I didn't let anything interfere with my dream."

Except for his rookie year in 1989, Jim's minor league batting averages from 1990 through 1993 never slipped below .313, except for one brief stint in Colorado Springs where he batted .285. Thome won two consecutive Lou Boudreau Awards, given annually to the top Cleveland Indians minor leaguer. Cleveland first brought Jim up to the majors in 1991 at the end of his second full minor-league season. He played in the minors again in 1992 and was again brought up at the end of the season. The following year, on August 13, 1993, he was brought up to the majors for good.

As a rookie, Jim—then a third baseman—topped all other American League hot sackers with 20 home runs. By 1996, Thome was the cream of the AL crop at the hot corner. He hit 38 round trippers to win the Silver Slugger Award. He also became only the third third baseman since 1953 to hit .300 with 100 RBIs and 30 home runs (Al Rosen and George Brett are the others).

Over the ensuing dozen years, Thome waged a relentless assault on the Cleveland record book. In '97, he became the first Indian ever to draw 100-plus walks while slamming 40 homers. He was the first Indian to string together back-to-back 100-plus walk seasons. In 1999, he wowed the crowd at Jacobs Field when he socked the park's longest-ever home run, a bomb that traveled 511 feet. He was sterling in the field, too. Jim boasted a nifty 46-game errorless streak at first base that season. In the postseason, he became the first player in major league history to sock two grand slams. In fact, his 17 career postseason

home runs (a ratio of one home run per 11.05 plate appearances) rank him third on the all-time list for post-season home runs.

You get the idea. Jim Thome is an immortal in Cleveland. He's in the same ranks with Feller, Averill, Lemon, and other great Indians. In his 2003 Phillie debut, Jim started a rapid ascent into the Phillies' Valhalla. He tied A-Rod for the major league lead in home runs (47). In doing so, he joined Ken Griffey Jr. as the only major leaguers ever to have back-to-back 40-home run seasons in different leagues. Jim also banged in 131 runs, third best in the NL, and the most RBIs by a Phillie since 1932. Jim finished fourth in MVP voting, which was the highest finish for a Phillie since Lenny Dykstra was runner-up to Barry Bonds in 1993.

In 2004, Thome slammed his 400th lifetime homer. "That was another night that showed what Jim Thome is about," Dan Stephenson cites. "The whole team had gotten champagne for him. It was on ice in the clubhouse, waiting for him to hit number 400. Naturally he hits it in his first at bat on the homestand. The game went into a rain delay. We didn't know it was officially called till two in the morning. But every guy hung around that clubhouse and congratulated Jim before the media was allowed in. Jim thanked everyone for staying around so long on his behalf. Then Todd Pratt, of all people, came up to Jim and said, 'Sure we stayed around. We love you, Jim.' The guys on the team think the world of Thome."

Jim Thome appears to be a cinch to reach the 500-homer plateau. He has the natural power to push well beyond that mark. He also possesses the discipline and prudent restraint to play the game at a high level for a long time. Jim works at keeping in shape.

"I'm a big guy, so I watch what I eat," Jim observes. "I love these Philly cheesesteaks, but I don't eat too many of them. I've got to keep focused on doing my job to the best of my ability."

Left: Jim Thome signs a baseball for young Phillies fan Ben Snyder before a 2004 home game. Thome's comfort with the Philly fan base was a factor in his decision to sign with the Phillies.
Doug Pensinger/Getty Images

MILT THOMPSON

"We called him 'Grandpop' in '93," former Phil Kim Batiste says of Milt Thompson. "Milt had been around longer than most of us. We had a great mix of veterans and young guys on that team. Milt kind of took the younger players under his wing and kept them moving in the right direction. He kept us out of trouble. I never had so much fun as I did on the '93 Phils team. Milt was a big reason for that and he was a big reason for our success. He was a quiet leader. He didn't have much to say, but he had a lot to add."

Milt put in two separate playing stints in Philly. He came up to the majors in the Atlanta Braves system. Atlanta had picked him second in the January, 1979 draft. "Grandpop" or "Scooter" as he was known in his earlier days, played for Savannah and Richmond in the minors. He debuted in the big leagues in 1984. He started 24 games for Atlanta that season, and hit .303 in 99 plate appearances. Despite his promising end-of-the-season performance, Milt was back at Richmond when the bell rang for the '85 season. He was called up again on July 5, 1985. In his first game back, he stroked three hits and threw out

Born: January 5, 1959, Washington D.C.
Position: Outfield
Years with the Phillies: 1986-1988; 1993-1994
Uniform Numbers: 24, 25
Major League Stats: .274, 47 HR, 357 RBI
Postseason Stats: 1993 NLCS: .231, 0 HR, 0 RBI; 1993 World Series: 313, 1 HR, 6 RBI

Left: A fan favorite during his two stints in Philadelphia as a player, Milt returned to the Phillies as a coach in 2003, working under Larry Bowa and Charlie Manuel.
Courtesy of the Philadelphia Phillies

two runners. This time around, he hit .302 in 182 appearances. His two consecutive .300 seasons weren't enough to keep him in Atlanta, however. On December 10, 1985, Milt, along with Steve Bedrosian, was peddled to the Phils for Ozzie Virgil and pitcher Pete Smith.

Milt started the '86 season with the Phils but was shipped to Portland on July 1. He burned up the minor leagues with a .341 average and 21 steals in 41 games before the Phils brought him back to stay. Milt answered with a .302 season in 1987. He followed with a .288 season in 1988. Those averages were tops on the Phils' roster both years. In '87, Milt also swiped a team-leading 46 bases. Nonetheless, in '89 he was shuttled off to St. Louis where his average exceeded .290 in three of his four seasons as a Cardinal.

"I came back to Philly in '93," Milt reflects. "I was happy to be back. For one thing, I loved

Philly fans. And for another, I had been playing baseball a long time but had never played in a postseason game. I felt we had a chance to go all the way in Philly in '93. We didn't have any single marquee player. We had a bunch of hungry guys who busted their butts every day to win. I've never seen that formula work so well as it did that year. I was proud to be a part of that team."

"Milt contributed more than his part," Ricky Jordan, Milt's teammate on the '93 team, adds. "We don't win anything that year without Milt's catch."

The catch came on April 29, 1993. The Phils were on a roll. The club had gotten off to the fastest start in its 110-year history. Philadelphia, as Philadelphians are wont to do, was waiting for the shoe to drop. The shoe appeared to be coming unlaced that day. Milt's three hits had helped push the Phils out to a shaky 5-3 lead. In the eighth inning, however, the Padres loaded the bases. Reliever David West was on the hill when the Padres' Bob Geren launched one high and deep to left—an apparent grand slam. Milt was off and running at the crack of the bat. He stood at the wall, timed his jump perfectly, stabbed his arm over the wall, and snagged the ball.

"That's the best catch I've ever seen," Mitch Williams reflects. "That was one of our biggest plays all year because it kept us rolling."

Milt gave an even grander performance in one of the Phillies' most fabled games—the 15-14 loss to Toronto in Game 4 of the Series.

"We were down 3-0 coming to bat in the bottom of the first," Milt remembers. "Stottlemyre [Toronto's pitcher] walked three guys ahead of me and forced a run in. When I came up, we were down 3-1 with two outs and the bases loaded. I got lucky and hit a triple to put us ahead 4-3."

"I'll tell you what a quality guy Milt Thompson is," Dan Stephenson points out. "In that game, Milt not only hit that triple. He also hit a double and single. He drove in five runs in one game—a Phillies World Series record. He needed a home run to become the first guy ever to hit for the cycle in a Series game. Milt confided to me that one of the biggest regrets in his entire career was swinging at the first pitch in his next at bat. He knew he had a shot at the cycle. He got overanxious and tried to jolt one out. Instead he made an easy out. Basically he let a personal thing influence his at-bat. Not many guys think that way. Not many guys today put the team ahead of themselves."

Milt ended the '93 season batting .262, but as Larry Bowa, a coach on the '93 squad put it, "It was as good a .262 as anyone could ever have. Milt came up big for us whenever we needed it. He was clutch in the field and at the plate."

Milt was a Phillie in '94 but age and injuries were catching up with him. He was hitting .273 that year when the Phils sent him to Houston late in the season. He played another year in Houston before splitting the 1996 season between the Los

> ## "Milt contributed more than his part. We don't win anything that year without Milt's catch."
>
> [RICKY JORDAN—FORMER PHILLIES FIRST BASEMAN]

Angeles and Colorado. After '96, Milt called it quits.

Since his retirement, Milt has served as a minor league outfield/ baserunner coordinator for both the Devil Rays and the Phils. He was also a coach at Reading for a couple of years. On September 30, 2003, he was named the Phillies first-base coach.

"A lot of ballplayers grouse when we ask them to do appearances and the like," Larry Shenk says. "Milt Thompson is the only ballplayer I've ever know who *asks* to go on our Phillies Winter Caravan. That's our wintertime PR thing where we visit several malls in several cities in the span of a week. Milt wants to improve his speaking ability and he welcomes the kind of public appearances the Caravan affords. That kind of thinking and acting is what suits him so well to coaching in the big leagues."

"Milt is low-key and quiet but he has the ability to get through to guys. He was instrumental in helping Jimmy Rollins to become a more complete player in 2004."

Milt batted over .300 four different times. He finished his pro career with a respectable .274 lifetime batting average. He currently resides in Williamstown, New Jersey. Milt and his wife, Rhonda, have four daughters: Torri, Brooke, Courtney, and Alyssa.

Left: Milt Thompson's leaping catch to rob San Diego's Bob Geren of a grand slam ignited the 1993 Phillies as they started their run to the pennant.
Stephen Dunn/Getty Images

MITCH WILLIAMS

There's a Philadelphia truism that goes like this. When you go back to your 10-year high school reunion, the kids who were always in trouble at school will now be policemen. They know all the angles firsthand. They can't be bamboozled. When Mitch Williams was named the pitching coach of the Atlantic City Surf, that old saw proved that it still had teeth.

As a player, Mitch Williams was the Phillies' Wild Thing. He was one closer who kept everyone on the edge of his or her seat.

"It was a high-wire act every time Mitch came into the game," Darren Daulton recalls. "But he got the job done. That's the bottom line. It wasn't pretty. It wasn't conventional, but it was entertaining as hell. He'd walk the first two guys. The crowd would be booing and screaming. I'd walk out to the mound and say, 'OK, you done screwin' around now?' Kruk would be yelling, 'Would you get this blankety-blank game over so I can get a beer?' Then, somehow he'd find a way out of trouble and we'd win."

Mitch is a natural-born entertainer. He's the kid who could never sit still in class, the class clown who was forever stirring a ruckus up.

Born: November 17, 1964, Santa Ana, Calif.
Position: Relief Pitcher
Years with the Phillies: 1991-1993
Uniform Number: 99
Major League Stats: 45-58, 3.65 ERA
Phillies Postseason Stats: 1993 NLCS: 2-0, 1.69 ERA; 1993 World Series: 0-2, 20.25 ERA (2-2/3 innings pitched)
Honors:
• NL Rolaids Pitcher of the Month June 1992
• NL All-Star as Cub in 1989
• NL Pitcher of the Week August 5-11, 1991
• August 1991 Pitcher of the Month

"You need two things to be a closer," Mitch insists. "A short memory and no brains. When it comes to having no brains, I'm a genius."

Mitch was the constant target of barbs from his own teammates. Those barbs were good-natured. Phillie fans, on the other hand, completely lost their sense of humor with Mitch after *THE* home run—the one Mitch served up to Joe Carter in Game 6 of the 1993 World Series. Carter smacked a Williams pitch over the left-field fence for a walk-off World Series–winning homer—only the second walk-off blast in the history of the

Left: Mitch Williams celebrates with catcher Darren Daulton after the Phillies beat the Braves for the National League Championship. His 43 saves in 1993 set a single-season Phillies record.
Courtesy of the Philadelphia Phillies

October Classic (Bill Mazeroski hit the first in 1960 when the Pirates beat the Yankees).

"We all felt bad for Mitch after that pitch," Terry Mulholland, a '93 Phillies All-Star pitcher reminisces. "Sure, he could drive you crazy because he never pitched a one-two-three inning. But Mitch left everything he had on the mound. We had such a great run in '93. I don't think any player on that team felt anything but pride for what we accomplished. We didn't get the story-

> ## "But Mitch left everything he had on the mound. We had such a great run in '93. I don't think any player on that team felt anything but pride for what we accomplished."
>
> [TERRY MULHOLLAND—FORMER PHILLIES STARTER]

book ending we wanted. But when it was over, we all felt worse for what happened to Mitch than we did about losing the Series."

"Mitch *did* have to endure a lot," broadcaster and '93 teammate Larry Andersen adds. "Our bullpen staff was all used up by the end of the season. As Fregosi put it, 'The relievers were barking.' Mitch had nothing left when he went into that game. But he took the ball and tried to get the job done. Most guys would have told Fregosi they had nothing left. Not Mitch. He wanted the ball every game.

"After that pitch to Carter, we all knew in our hearts Mitch wouldn't be back in Philly next year. It was awful what the guy had to go through—the death threats and fan backlash.

Mitch was a stand-up guy, though. He could take it and rebound. Mitch never made excuses. But I'll tell you a secret. Remember, there was some guy who threw eggs at Mitch's house? They finally found out who it was. It was Mitch—he was aiming at the neighbor's house."

No one ever resists joking about Mitch. Nor can Mitch resist a good prank. That's why the news of Mitch's new career as pitching coach was so startling.

Before Tug McGraw died, he spoke about Mitch. "Mitch and I were two different people," Tug said. "We each got the job done. We just did it in different ways. I knew I couldn't overpower anyone. I had to rely on fooling hitters. The Phils asked me to try to work with Mitch. They wanted me to teach him some other pitches—how to change speeds and how to keep batters off balance. Mitch told me, 'I appreciate your help, Tug, but honestly, I can't pitch that way. The way I've always done it is to rear back and fire. That's what I do and that's what I'll continue to do till I can't do it anymore. And then I'll walk away from the game.' "

Lost amid the spectacle of his Joe Carter nightmare and his own reputation as a flake was the fact that Mitch had a solid career studded with some stellar achievements.

San Diego drafted Mitch in the eighth round of the 1982 June draft. He burst onto the big league scene with characteristic fury. Mitch came up in 1986 as a Texas Ranger. He had a great debut, setting an all-time rookie record for appearances and leading the American League in games pitched. He fanned 90 batters in 98 innings. Of course, he wasn't called the Wild Thing capriciously. He also issued 78 free passes. He finished with a 3.58 ERA and an 8-6 record, which he reprised the following season. His ERA as a sophomore dropped to 3.23. He also whiffed an impressive 129 batters in 108 2/3 frames. His 1.19 strikeouts/innings pitched ratio was second best in the AL. His 85 mound appearances also ranked second in the junior circuit. That season he became the third pitcher in ML history and first ever in the AL to pitch in at least 80 games in consecutive seasons. Opposing batters hit a measly .175 against him in '87—lowest in the majors.

In his third season, he slipped to 2-7. His ERA ballooned to 4.63. The Rangers dealt him to the Cubs in a multi-player deal. The Wild Thing packed for the Windy City along with lefties Steve Wilson and Paul Kilgus, infielders Luis Benitez and Curt Wilkerson, and outfielder Pablo Delgado. In return, the Cubs sent lefties Drew Hall and Jamie Moyer along with Rafael Palmeiro to Texas.

Mitch led the NL (and tied for the ML lead) in appearances in his first season as a Cub. He became the fifth pitcher in history to lead in appearances in both the AL and NL. He placed second in saves (36) and games finished (61) and was chosen to the All-Star team. Mitch pitched one inning in the mid-summer classic. He walked one, struck out one, and didn't allow a run.

Mitch was going great guns in 1990 until he injured his knee covering first base in early June. The injury required arthroscopic surgery and he was out of action for a month. He finished the season with a horrendous 1-8 record.

In 1991, on the eve of opening day, the Phils sent two pitchers, Chuck McElroy and Bob Scanlon, to the Cubbies for the Wild Thing. In his Phillies debut season, Mitch finished second in

the NL in games finished (60), third in winning percentage (70.6 percent, based on a 12-5 record), tied for third in saves, and tied for ninth in appearances. His ERA was a team-best, career-best 2.34. Mitch sizzled that August. He went 8-1 to set the ML record for most wins by a reliever in a month.

Mitch slipped to 5-8, 3.78 in 1992 but recharged in 1993. His 43 saves for the pennant-winners broke the Phils' record for saves in a season, which had been set by Cy Young winner Steve Bedrosian. Bedrock saved 40 in 1987. Jose Mesa now holds the club's mark. "Joe Table" bested Mitch's record in 2002.

Mitch ran out of bullets after the Carter episode. The Wild Thing played for Houston, California, and Kansas City in '94, '95, and '97. His ERAs were successively 7.65, 6.75, and 10.80—which skewed and swelled an otherwise fine career ERA to 3.65.

After his playing days, Mitch opened a bowling alley. He later opened a restaurant in Veterans Stadium with partner and ex-teammate John Kruk. The duo hosted a radio program for awhile. Then as the new millennium swept in, the shocking, are-you-sure-about-that news that Mitch was pitching coach for the Atlantic City Surf rocked Phillytown. Mitch did so well in his stint as pitching coach that he was promoted to manager in 2002. He has since left. As of this writing, the Wild Thing has not settled on anything new. Stay tuned. He will.

The most unique thing about this unique character is his current status with the allegedly unforgiving fans of Philly. Unlike Bill Buckner, Ralph Branca, and others who had landed on misfortune's whoopie cushion, Mitch has been accepted by the Phillies faithful. He always gets one of the loudest cheers when he comes back to Phillie events. But then, did you ever notice that the same thing happens to the bad guys at a high school reunion?

Celebrate the Heroes of Philadelphia and Pennsylvania Sports in These Other Releases from Sports Publishing!

Walking Together Forever: The Broad Street Bullies, Then and Now
by Jim Jackson

• 6 x 9 hardcover
• 250 pages
• photos throughout
• $24.95 • 2005 release!

Eagles: Where Have You Gone?
by Fran Zimniuch

• 6 x 9 hardcover
• 250 pages
• photos throughout
• $24.95

Phillies: Where Have You Gone?
by Fran Zimniuch

• 6 x 9 hardcover
• 200 pages
• photos throughout
• $24.95

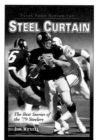

Tales from Behind the Steel Curtain
by Jim Wexell

• 5.5 x 8.25 hardcover
• 200 pages
• photos throughout
• $19.95

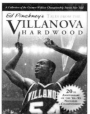

Ed Pinckney's Tales from the Villanova Hardwood
by Ed Pinckney
with Bob Gordon

• 5.5 x 8.25 hardcover
• 200 pages
• photos throughout
• $19.95

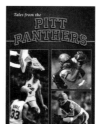

Tales from the Pitt Panthers
by Sam Sciullo Jr.

• 5.5 x 8.25 hardcover
• 200 pages
• photos throughout
• $19.95

Jameer
by Floyd "Pete" Nelson and Elaine Whelan

• 5.5 x 8.25 hardcover
• 170 pages
• photos throughout
• $19.95

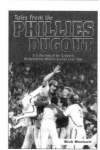

Tales from the Phillies Dugout
by Rich Westcott

• 5.5 x 8.25 hardcover
• 200 pages
• photos throughout
• $19.95

Roethlisberger: Pittsburgh's Own Big Ben
by Sports Publishing L.L.C.

• 8.5 x 11 trade paper
• 128 pages
• color photos throughout
• $14.95
• 2005 release!

More than Beards, Bellies and Biceps: The Story of the 1993 Phillies
by Robert Gordon and Tom Burgoyne

• 6 x 9 hardcover
• 225 pages
• eight-page photo section
• $22.95

To order at any time, please call toll-free **877-424-BOOK (2665)**.
For fast service and quick delivery, order on-line at **www.SportsPublishingLLC.com**